AT A FOREIGN UNIVERSITY

An International Study of Adaptation and Coping

Otto Klineberg
W. Frank Hull IV

PRAEGER

PRAEGER SPECIAL STUDIES • PRAEGER SCIENTIFIC

Library of Congress Cataloging in Publication Data

Klineberg, Otto, 1899-
   At a foreign university.

   Bibliography: p.
   Includes index.
   1. Foreign study. 2. Student adjustment.
I. Hull, William Frank, 1941-   joint author.
II. Title.
LB2375.K54   378.1'98   79-18170
ISBN 0-03-052486-5

Published in 1979 by Praeger Publishers
A Division of Holt, Rinehart and Winston/CBS, Inc.
383 Madison Avenue, New York, New York 10017 U.S.A.

9 038 987654321

Printed in the United States of America

INTERNATIONAL COMMITTEE FOR THE STUDY OF EDUCATIONAL EXCHANGE

Chairman:
Vernon I. Cheadle, Chancellor Emeritus, University of California
  at Santa Barbara

Members:
Guilardo Martins Alves, former President, Council of Rectors of
  Brazilian Universities
Asa Briggs, Provost, Worcester College, Oxford
Lameck Goma, Vice Chancellor, University of Zambia
Theodore M. Hesburgh, President, University of Notre Dame
Wolf Isselhard, former Rector, University of Cologne
Alex Kwapong, former Vice Chancellor, University of Ghana;
  Vice Rector, United Nations University
Choh-Ming Li, former Vice Chancellor, Chinese University of
  Hong Kong
Felipe E. MacGregor, Rector, Pontifical Catholic University of
  Peru
R. C. Mehrotra, Vice Chancellor, University of Delhi
Sukenaga Murai, former President, Waseda University
Houshang Nahavandi, former Chancellor, University of Teheran
Jean Roche, former Rector, University of Paris
Ivan Supek, former Rector, University of Zagreb
Ron Watts, Principal, Queens University at Kingston

Research Directors:
Otto Klineberg; Paris, France, <u>Director</u>
W. Frank Hull IV; Portland, Oregon, <u>Deputy Director</u>

ACKNOWLEDGEMENTS

The authors express their sincere gratitude to the following organizations and individuals:

The Aquinas Fund, the former U.S. Department of State Bureau of Educational and Cultural Affairs and its director Mr. Richard Roth, Mrs. Harold F. Sheets, the Asian Foundation, the W. F. Hewlett Foundation, and the Frank Freiman Charitable Trust, for their generous financial support of this international investigation.

The International Social Science Council and the International Union of Psychological Sciences for helpful financial contributions. It should be added that the views expressed in this volume are not necessarily those of the international organizations involved.

The University of California at Santa Barbara, office of the Chancellor, and particularly the former chancellor, Vernon I. Cheadle, and the present chancellor, R. Huttenback, for continuing support.

The Rockefeller Foundation for its hospitality at Bellagio, which permitted us to make definite decisions regarding methodology.

The Council on International Educational Exchange, and particularly John Bowman and Jack Egle, for constant encouragement and administrative assistance.

Richard Ting-Ku Houang, for his valuable help with the computer and the statistical analysis of our data.

G. V. Coelho and W. E. Allaway, for valuable suggestions during the earlier stages of the investigation.

Elijah P. Lovejoy, for helpful critical comments on the text.

George P. Zimmar of the Praeger Publishers, for his cooperation in the final stages of preparation for publication.

Our senior research colleagues and associates in various countries: Michael Kendall, Judy M. Powell, and Edwin H. Cox in the United Kingdom; Prem Pasricha and Dr. and Mrs. S. Chandrasekhar in India; M. Nassefat and B. Saroukhani in Iran; W. E. Lambert in Canada; K. Onuma, M. Yamashira, and Chiyoko Kobayshi in Japan; Arrigo L. Angelini in Brazil; Peter Tam in Hong Kong; Axel Markert and J. K. Janes in the Federal Republic of Germany.

Kevin P. Finney, for his work in the coding and tabulation of our data.

Our secretaries, Brigitte Vidé in Paris and Sylvia C. Dunning and Fawn D. Miller in Santa Barbara.

Cheryl A. Kelly, for the typing and retyping of our manu-script and notes.

Last, but far from least, the many students and senior scholars in 11 countries who answered our questions and submitted to our interviews.

CONTENTS

LIST OF TABLES

1

INTRODUCTION:
THE CONTEXT OF
THE PRESENT STUDY

The direct stimulation and encouragement to carry out the present investigation came to the authors of this volume from the International Committee for the Study of Educational Exchange, and particularly from its chairman, Vernon I. Cheadle. This Committee, consisting of present or former heads of universities in 13 different countries and Hong Kong, had a common interest in programs of international educational exchanges and also shared a conviction that there is a need for research in order to determine the impact of such exchanges and the degree to which the relevant goals are being realized. Plans for the research were developed at a series of preliminary meetings of the Committee, and the decision to proceed was taken in Montreal in 1970. It was understood from the outset that the projected investigation was to be international in character and was to be based on findings obtained through the cooperation of scholars from a number of different countries. It was hoped that two types of publications would result; on the one hand, a volume which would be based on cross-national comparisons, for the purpose of identifying both similarities and differences in the experience with international exchanges, and, on the other, a series of separate reports on the situation within each country.

The research was to be carried out in two distinct though interrelated stages. The first was to concentrate on what was happening, with the following questions in mind: What were different universities and different countries doing in this connection? What administrative arrangements were involved? Who went abroad, and for what purpose; and who came _from_ abroad? What problems were encountered, and what measures were taken in the attempt to solve them? The research during the second stage was to concern itself with the effects of international exchanges on the students and faculties concerned. Did they consider their foreign sojourn to be a success or a failure? Why? What difficulties did they face, and how did they surmount them? What suggestions did they have for the improvement of exchange programs? What practical implications emerged with regard to the administration of such programs?

A volume dealing with the first stage of the project has already been published.[1] It includes summaries of reports received from colleagues in seven different countries (France, the Federal Republic of Germany, India, Japan, the United Kingdom, the United States, and Yugoslavia) in each of which there was an account of the situation in one particular university as well as in the country as a whole. An introductory section of the book dealt with cross-national comparisons, and the final chapter attempted to draw the conclusions and implications that the data appeared to justify. There was also an indication as to further research which, in the judgment of the author and his colleagues, should be undertaken. The suggestions included, among others, greater emphasis on international or cross-cultural comparisons; more concern with exchanges at the faculty level in terms of both their immediate and long-term consequences; a study of those individuals who are eager to go abroad and those who are indifferent or even hostile to the idea; an analysis of the mental health implications of exchanges as well as of academic success or failure among foreign students. It was these concerns which led the way to the present investigation, although obviously not all of them could be adequately explored at the same time.

In our discussions with university administrators involved in exchange programs as well as with other colleagues and also with foundation executives to whom we appealed for financial support, we encountered two contrasting attitudes. One was to the effect that there had already been enough research on this problem, and that it would be sufficient to draw out the practical implications of what had already been discovered. Adherents of the other view said that there was still a lot to learn and that our investigation deserved encouragement. We ourselves would admit that in terms of what was already available in the extensive literature, a considerable number of specific practical suggestions could be made which, if taken seriously, would be helpful both to administrators and participants in exchange programs. We were convinced, however, that something further was needed, and we planned the present investigation in the hope that we might make a contribution toward the identification and understanding of some previously neglected aspects of this important problem.

Before we describe our own investigation, we should like to add a word about the "extensive literature" to which reference was made above. We are familiar with the definition of originality as consisting of not knowing what anyone else has said or written before you. We have done our best to acquaint ourselves with what our colleagues in a number of countries have published, and our debt to them is great. Obviously, we have not read everything that has been written, but the fact that both of us have been concerned with these issues over a considerable number of years gives us the hope that we have not neglected anything of crucial importance. It is clear in any case that without some knowledge of the issues that others have raised, and the hypotheses that they have explored, our own study could not have been planned or executed.

We shall not make the attempt at this stage to summarize the content of the available literature, or to present an adequate bibliography. At various points throughout this report, we have included references related to the particular issues under consideration. For readers who are interested in a more complete listing, a number of recent surveys are available.[2]

As far as this particular study is concerned, our claim to have contributed something new in spite of all that has already been published rests upon the following considerations.

1. Ours is a truly <u>international</u> investigation, in which the same techniques were applied and the same questions asked of our respondents in a number of different countries. The research conducted in the past has dealt overwhelmingly with the situation as it affects the United States, involving mainly American investigators. The earlier study under the aegis of the International Committee for the Study of Educational Exchange, and which was briefly described above, involved the comparison of experiences in seven countries. In the present investigation, we are able to report on data obtained in 11 countries—Brazil, Canada, the Federal Republic of Germany, France, Hong Kong, India, Iran, Japan, Kenya, the United Kingdom, and the United States.

This is certainly the most extensive cross-national study of university exchanges ever conducted. To our knowledge, the only previous international comparison is to be found in the report by Eide[3] in which she reports the results of an ingenious research design dealing with "students as links between cultures." Eide compared the reactions of students from three different "developing" countries (Egypt, India, and Iran) who had studied abroad in one of three technically "advanced" countries (the Federal Republic of Germany, the United Kingdom, and the United States). The data were collected by local social scientists in the three "developing" countries.

This was certainly an excellent study, but it was focused primarily on a problem of particular interest to the United Nations Educational, Scientific and Cultural Organization (UNESCO), namely, on students as links in the relationships between cultures. We regard this as a very important issue, but our own research instruments included a much greater range of topics as well as a more extensive geographical distribution.

The number of countries covered permitted a wider range of cross-cultural comparisons than anyone else has so far attempted; moreover, in the case of some countries, this book marks the very first occasion on which research on their international exchanges had ever been conducted. This is true, to the best of our knowledge, for Brazil, Hong Kong, and Kenya; it is also true for Japan, except for its participation in the Committee's earlier study. In this connection, we would like to repeat our hope that the investigators in each of the countries concerned will themselves publish locally and in their own language the results of their own particular portion of the total investigation. Our colleagues in Brazil, Canada, India, and Iran have already informed us that this is their intention. For the United States, this has already been done,[4] and the report on the American results can usefully be read in conjunction with the present volume.

2. Our questionnaire has not only been applied internationally; it has been <u>constructed internationally</u>. We wished at all costs to avoid the widespread tendency for a questionnaire to be designed in one country by one group of investigators, and then sent to colleagues elsewhere with a request that they apply it in their own country. Instead, we held an eight-day meeting in Bellagio, Italy in August 1974 during which the individual items in the questionnaire were developed and intensively discussed with participants from Brazil, Canada, the Federal Republic of Germany, France, Ghana, Hong Kong, Japan, the United Kingdom, the United States, and Yugoslavia. Items were retained only if all those present agreed that they could be meaningfully applied in their own country. Unfortunately, it was impossible to obtain data from Ghana and Yugoslavia, but three other countries were later added, namely India, Iran, and Kenya.

3. The questionnaire was designed to be as <u>comprehensive</u> as possible, and to permit the establishment of <u>interrelationships</u> among the various factors that might affect the adaptation or coping process during the foreign sojourn. We are not the first to attempt this type of analysis, but we believe that the scope of our questionnaire made it possible for us to identify certain of these interrelationships more clearly; in any case, we certainly analyzed these in a wider geographical context than has been done before. Our goal in this connection, for example, was not only to report on degree of satisfaction, experience of prejudice and discrimination, contact with the local population, problems related to finances and housing, depression and homesickness, and so on, but also to investigate the correspondences or relationships between the responses made in these areas, and further to determine whether the same correspondences were found in different national samples (Chapter 11).

4. The study was directed also toward the consideration, in the light of our data, of certain <u>hypotheses</u> that emerge from previous research, and to an indication of <u>how probable</u> these hypotheses appear to be in an international context. To anticipate what will be discussed more fully below, our findings, for example, support the emphasis that has been placed on the importance of friendly social contact with the host population (Chapter 5); on the other hand, they cast considerable doubt on the validity of the concept of the U-curve (Chapter 9).

5. In addition to the questionnaire, presented at one particular point in the sojourn of a foreign student, we also made use of <u>personal interviews.</u> In the case of students (as contrasted with faculty members, to be discussed below), we conducted three interviews with a relatively small but varied sample. The first interview occurred shortly after the beginning of the academic year; the second, about midway through the year; the third, toward the end. Our purpose was to look at the foreign sojourn as a miniature life history which would enable us to see more clearly the gradual process of adaptation to the new environment and the success (or occasional failure) in coping with the difficulties that arise (Chapters 4, 7, and 8).

6. In the first study made under the auspices of the Committee,[5] it was suggested that more research should be undertaken at the <u>faculty</u> level, during the foreign sojourn and in retrospect. We decided as part of the present study to include faculty (interpreted rather broadly to cover teachers and researchers at various levels of seniority, such as former Fulbright scholars or those who had had other types of fellowships of a comparable character); we submitted a questionnaire to a varied sample, and interviewed a smaller number 10 to 15 years after they had been abroad. The report on Americans who have had this experience has already been published.[6] Our decision to use a retrospective or long-term approach was based on our feeling that enough time should have elapsed to give the participants adequate perspective in their judgment of the consequences of the foreign sojourn, and also to allow any possible "sleeper effect"[7] to have exerted its influence. There are some reports in the literature along these lines,[8] but the topics we covered were quite different from the earlier ones; in any case, our respondents covered a much wider geographical range.

Because of the features just described, we feel that we have the right to say that our investigation differs in a number of significant aspects from any that can be found in previous publications. We had to face a number of difficulties, which is not too surprising in the case of an investigation involving so many different countries. The number of foreign students, for example, who answered the questionnaires varied greatly from one country to another, the result being much larger samples from the United States, the United Kingdom, and Canada than from other countries. (The exact size of all the samples is reported on below.) The same holds for the retrospective study of the more senior subjects.

While the interviews were conducted in all the countries involved, they were not all presented in a comparable manner or with similar content. We have, of course, examined them all and have made use of as many as possible. We have in all cases reported on the source of every interview included in our analysis. In some instances, we have looked at our total foreign student population, one example being our presentation of the interrelationships among the various items of our questionnaire (Chapter 11). We have done something similar in the discussion of the long-term impact of a foreign sojourn in the case of more senior scholars (Chapter 7). The data always include, however, the differences found among the individual country samples as well as the more global analyses. We grant that there is no such thing as the foreign student, but we were interested in discovering whether there were any common, or at least usual, experiences related to the foreign sojourn in general and to the varied situations met with in different countries.

NOTES

1. Otto Klineberg, International Educational Exchange (Paris: Mouton, 1976).

2. Seth Spaulding, Michael Flack, et al., The World's Students in the United States (New York: Praeger, 1976), contains an extensive annotated bibliography. References to studies conducted not only in the United States but also in other countries will be found in Ingrid Eide, ed., Students as Links between Cultures (Oslo: Universitetsforlaget, 1970), particularly in the chapters by Marshall and Breitenbach, and also in Otto Klineberg, "International Exchanges in Education, Science and Culture," Social Sciences Information 4, no. 4 (1966): 91-143.

3. Eide, op. cit.

4. W. Frank Hull IV, Foreign Students in the United States of America: Coping Behavior within the Educational Environment (New York: Praeger, 1978).

5. Klineberg, International Educational Exchange.

6. W. Frank Hull IV and Walter H. Lemke, Jr., "Retrospective Assessment of the United States Senior Fulbright-Hays Program," International Educational and Cultural Exchange 13, no. 2 (Spring 1978): 6-9.

7. C. D. Hovland, A. A. Lumsdaine, and F. D. Sheffield, Experiments on Mass Communication (Princeton: Princeton University Press, 1949).

8. See John Useem and Ruth H. Useem, The Western-Educated Man in India (New York: Dryden, 1955); and Eide, op. cit.

2

METHODOLOGICAL
CONSIDERATIONS

Over the past several years, many individuals in various nations around the world, both within and outside of educational institutions, have found that systematic information on the adaptation and coping of foreign students within institutions of post-secondary education is not available. Admissions criteria and past credentials are not always the most comprehensive indicators of the students' ability to complete programs successfully in a foreign institution. The goal for which they enter an educational institution—the attainment of a degree, a diploma, or a credential that provides a means to further ends—is likely to be influenced by a whole host of factors in their background and in the particular situation and reception that they perceive at the foreign institution. It should be noted that the term "perceive" used here is a crucial one. The perception of a student may or may not correspond closely to reality. Nevertheless, what influences the students and their progress toward their goal will very much be related to what is perceived or felt at the host institution in its total milieu: the faculty, the fellow students, the staff, the townspeople, the physical environment, and so forth.

All of us involved in international educational exchange certainly want foreign students—indeed, we want all students—to be successful and to attain credentials permitting them to reach self-satisfying goals and levels in life. Very few of us would seriously argue that such success can be predicted on the basis of application data and test scores alone. Certainly, those clearly unable to accomplish the academic work at the assumed educational level can be prevented from entering the foreign institution, but there will always be many applicants who should not have been permitted to enter, and there will always be students who are denied admission but would have succeeded admirably if they had been given the chance. Beyond admissions criteria, there are a host of variables playing a crucial—some might say the crucial—role in the success or failure of a student's reaching the goal of attaining the credential and moving forward. These other variables are related to the process of coping and adaptation in the foreign university environment. What are the aspects of personal experience during the sojourn which lead to positive coping as well as a realization of the cognitive and personal objectives that brought the foreign student to the host institution? While others have attempted to answer this question in part, the emphasis of the present investigation—as we have said in Chapter 1—is on international data and methodological uniformity, enabling us to present an international analysis of a problem faced by nations representing widely differing cultures in many different parts of the world.

The authors realize that there is a certain trauma inherent in the adjustment made by students when they transfer from a secondary or high school to a college or university even when they merely leave one section of the hometown and travel to its other side. There are adjustment problems faced in residence halls, the round-the-clock influence of peers for better or for worse, and so forth. It is also true that students leaving a relatively rural and close-knit community for a major, impersonal university located in a metropolitan area in another section of their own country will encounter adjustment difficulties and will need to establish patterns for coping and adaptation early in the transition. Yet it is our opinion that special attention should be paid to the adaptation process undergone by those students who journey from one foreign country to another in search of an education. One might argue that the stakes are higher, that foreign students are risking more by entering a culture which may be full of particular customs that are unknown and unanticipated. It is more important, however, to recognize that in studying the coping and adaptation process internationally, we are really studying a process inherent in any institution within any country but in a context where the difficulties may be expected to be more apparent, and where the process might be more easily visible.

Based on previous research and a great deal of prior planning, the actual design of this present investigation began to take form when 15 scholars and researchers representing ten countries from around the world met for eight days in Bellagio, Italy in August 1974, as was mentioned earlier.

All of those attending were knowledgeable about the problems and successes of foreign students in their own respective areas of the world. All were concerned about the foreign sojourn and were prepared to contribute from their personal areas of expertise toward an approach that would be workable, sound, and practical. During

those eight days, detailed instruments, including particular items
and response options, were drafted and openly discussed again and
again. The end result was an international, interdisciplinary approach to studying the sojourn experience as well as a detailed draft
of a document, or instrument, to be pilot tested.

Over the next year and a half, detailed pilot studies were
conducted and/or specific comments on the methodology as well as
new items were submitted from Brazil, Canada, France, Ghana,
Hong Kong, Iran, Japan, and the United States. Some items were
reworded again and again, and the order of the items was altered.
Often changes were made for reasons of communication, sometimes
because of translation problems. Academic calendars had to be considered and plans established in a way that would be workable in
each participating country. Senior research personnel with experience and expertise in this particular area were invited to collect the
data. The pilot studies were conducted between September 1974 and
March 1976. However, professional input into the process continued
through July 1976, at which point the methodology and instruments
were put into final form by the two of us who served as directors of
the project as a whole.

Throughout this process, it was imperative to be aware that
we did not wish to adopt a Western, an Asian, or any other ethnocentric approach. Various academic specialities were represented
and various theories were proposed. All the researchers, scholars,
and consultants shared equally in the input for this project. Everyone did not agree with the particular wording of every item, but what
was accepted finally was precisely what was sought: an international
and interdisciplinary methodology for the study of coping and adaptation of students at foreign universities.

The methodology for the investigation had to take into account
several important realities characteristic of international investigations:

1. The methodology had to be as clear and simple as possible
to make it less liable to error or misunderstanding by the foreign
student respondents, and to make it more feasible for the investigation to be conducted in various countries where financial and human
resources for research are exceedingly limited.

2. The emphasis in the study had to be on selecting competent and capable senior foreign researchers in each country and
utilizing their personal judgments in choosing varied student samples
within that country rather than insisting on the rigid methodological
and experimental controls ideally required for representative sampling. Strict experimental procedures for sampling are simply not
always possible or even appropriate for an investigation at the

international level. Decisions and adaptations had to be made on the spot and had to be under the direction of a qualified local senior researcher at the foreign study site in question.

3. The instruments, or questionnaires, had to be restricted in length so as to increase the likelihood of the respondents' cooperation. Not everything could be covered; rather, the instruments were built upon past research and experience and then made as concise as possible. The instrument used contained 155 items, the English version of which numbered 16 pages. Whenever possible, the foreign students were offered the instrument in the language which they best understood, but in most cases it was completed in the language of instruction of the school in which the student was studying.

4. The focus of the investigation was in part on the foreign student sojourn as a form of clinical life history. Thus, specific attention was paid to case studies which followed the development of the newly arrived foreign student during the first academic year. The purpose of the case studies was not just to supplement the hard data available from the main instrument, but to focus attention on the coping process as well as on four major themes: sources of satisfaction, difficulties encountered, changes in attitudes, and suggestions for improving the foreign sojourn experience.

As for the main investigation, during months five through seven (mid-year) of the academic year, beginning in 1976 through 1977 depending on local conditions and academic calendars, we sent questionnaires to samples of nonimmigrant foreign students (as determined by passport regulations for the foreign country in question) enrolled at study institutions within each country. The order of items and the items themselves were as identical as translation procedures permitted. Great care was taken to insure effective and clear communication. For example, the directions and introductory materials for students in Iran were printed in two columns: one in Parsi, the other in English. It must be stressed that the local senior researcher directed and supervised the data collection in each foreign country in order to secure the clearest possible record of foreign student opinion in each country.

At the same time, as soon as possible after the start of the academic year, a sample of 20 newly arriving nonimmigrant foreign students was randomly selected at study institutions in each foreign country. Those 20 students were interviewed at the beginning, at the middle, and at the close of the academic year. The purpose of the interviews was to produce clear case studies descriptive of each individual's coping and adjustment process and of the mechanisms utilized by each student through the initial academic year at the foreign university. During the interviews, attention was directed to all areas covered in the instrument as well as to any other situations encountered by the individual students during the academic year that seemed to have an influence on their coping and adjustment. Again the interviews were conducted in the language of instruction at the host institution, but in some cases where particular students felt more comfortable in another language, the interviews were conducted in that language. All interviews were under the direct supervision of the local senior researcher who was responsible for the actual conducting of the interviews within the guidelines, training, and direction provided by the international directors of the investigation; for example, interviewers were instructed to talk with the student about his experiences but to be prepared to probe more deeply at any point where there were problems or difficulties, in order to obtain an understanding of what was happening to him. In the case of poor grades or decisions to drop out of the institution, the interviewers were instructed to probe for the antecedents, seeking opinions from faculty as well as secretaries who had had contact with such students.

In many cases, the interviewers and the students became friends over the course of that year. While only three interviews were formally scheduled, many interviewers met more frequently with the students for a "cup of coffee" or just to stay in touch. Interviewers were encouraged to contact professors and any others who might be able to supply as many unobtrusive behavioral indications as possible regarding what was happening to the foreign students. The objective was to provide as complete a picture as possible of their situation in the foreign university throughout the initial academic year.

As the investigation progressed, the international directors remained in as close touch as possible with the respective researchers and their support staffs in each participating country. There were long telephone calls, visits, and a great deal of correspondence; but in the end, the effectiveness of the choice of the samples in each country, their representativeness, and the completeness of the case studies, were the responsibility of those researchers in each country who had undertaken these difficult and demanding tasks. In almost all countries, the senior researchers were full members of the faculty concerned, with doctorates and long years of experience. In two cases, administrative personnel with appropriate experience served as local senior researchers.

All instruments were transmitted to the office of one of the authors at the University of California at Santa Barbara and were there coded, key punched, verified, and placed into the University's computer. All case studies were also transmitted to the same office after having been translated into English by the local foreign researcher in charge; they were then copied and studied by both authors.

Thus, while the data collection procedures were supervised and controlled within the methodological guidelines by those senior local researchers at the study sites, the analyses were centrally conducted. The data reported on in this volume include all those that had been received from the participating countries at the University of California at Santa Barbara by June 15, 1978. Brazil, Canada, the Federal Republic of Germany, France, Hong Kong, India, Iran, Japan, Kenya, the United Kingdom, and the United States were all represented in this investigation.

A few further words may be appropriate with regard to the samples collected in each participating country. The countries themselves were invited to participate on the basis of: (1) the presence of foreign students available for study in their institutions, (2) the availability of senior research personnel experienced in undertaking such research and data collection as well as knowledgeable and interested in the areas under study, and (3) an adequate geographical distribution of countries from all areas of the world. More or fewer countries could have been included, but the intent was to keep the investigation within manageable proportions while retaining a high level of professional expertise among the selected senior researchers. Regrettably, plans to include a country from the Communist world were not realized.

Once local senior researchers were selected and the cooperation of key institutions ensured, a great deal of time was spent by the international directors to make certain that the details of the investigation were understood by those senior researchers who had not been previously involved in the planning. Everyone recognized that it was impossible to survey all nonimmigrant foreign students in any participating country. Furthermore, there is no experimental and practical way to guarantee that we end up with a completely representative number or type of institutions or students through techniques applicable internationally to all the countries in question. Cost factors also entered here. In any case, the most technically precise sample in any given country is unsatisfactory if it does not take into account the spread and diversity of students studying in that country.

The actual sampling of foreign students enrolled within institutions in participating countries and the planning of the sampling were almost solely under the direction and decision of the local senior researchers. While the international directors paid careful attention to the selection of the educational institutions that were to participate in the sampling procedures, and assisted when appropriate, a tremendous amount of thought and effort was required of the local senior researchers in order to produce a varied sample of foreign students in the country in question; indeed, each sample produced enabled the investigator to say, "Yes, this is a fair sample of the foreign students studying in my country and a sample that we may professionally consider representative in my best judgment." More than that, no one could demand.

For the specialist in statistical research, our samples do not always fulfill ideal requirements. Some do; some do not. A more detailed presentation of data collection and sampling procedures illustrative of the techniques used is available for the project conducted within the United States.[1]

We have done our best to produce samples in each of the countries that can reasonably be considered representative of the nonimmigrant foreign student populations studying in these countries. While no statistical picture of any international populations can ever claim to be completely reliable for all times and for all purposes, we have studied the samples produced by the local senior researchers in each of the participating countries, and we feel that we have a reasonable basis for presenting a graphic description and analysis of coping and adaptation in the countries in question and can deal adequately with the variables under study.

The 2,536 respondents included in this analysis were studying in the following countries: Brazil, 149; Canada, 620; the Federal Republic of Germany, 42; France, 96; Hong Kong, 42; India, 56; Iran, 73; Japan, 30; Kenya, 84; the United Kingdom, 370; and the United States, 955.

NOTE

1. W. Frank Hull IV, Foreign Students in the United States of America: Coping Behavior within the Educational Environment (New York: Praeger, 1978).

3

THE STUDENT POPULATION

In the present chapter, we will first describe the general characteristics of the student population; we will also indicate the countries in which our investigations were conducted, the origins of the students in our samples, their disciplinary interests, and other aspects necessary for understanding the nature of the population. In the second part of this chapter, we discuss the general impressions reported by these students with regard to their sojourn as a whole, and make special reference to their judgments of the teaching quality at the institutions that they attended.

CHARACTERISTICS

The 2,536 student respondents who completed lengthy questionnaire instruments for this investigation were all nonimmigrant foreign students (as determined by passport regulations for the country in question) enrolled at institutions of post-secondary education, as previously indicated, in Brazil, Canada, the Federal Republic of Germany, Hong Kong, India, Iran, Japan, Kenya, the United Kingdom, and the United States. The students were asked to complete the instruments between months five through seven (mid-year) of the academic calendars beginning in 1976 through 1977. As different institutions in various countries utilize distinctly different academic calendars and as local conditions varied, some of the foreign students responded as early as January 1977, others as late as the first months of 1978. The data utilized for the analyses consisted of all completed questionnaires received as of June 15, 1978, at the University of California at Santa Barbara.

Of the respondents, most were males, with an average age between 23 and 27, depending upon the country in question (see Table 3.1). Older students were more likely to be studying in Japan or in the United States. Most of the respondents indicated that they had lived the longest within urban backgrounds prior to their sojourn, one exception being those in Kenya, where 74 percent of the sample came from a rural background. The greatest percentage of the samples tended to have stayed in the sojourn country for more than two years, with the exception of those studying in Hong Kong and Kenya, the tenure of these students being from one to four months and from five to eight months respectively. The amount of previous formal study completed by the respondents since finishing secondary school and prior to the sojourn varied by country, ranging from those in India who averaged 2.1 years, to 4.6 years for those in Hong Kong, and 4.5 years in the United States.

Respondents were asked to select the disciplinary area that most closely represented their previous studies. Our purpose was to obtain an indication of academic disciplinary areas of interest. This permitted the respondents to self-select those disciplinary areas with which they most closely identified themselves. For the total study population, the respondents were in the following categories: engineering and physical sciences, 35 percent; behavioral and social sciences, 20 percent; arts and humanities, 18 percent; biological and life sciences, 15 percent; and other areas of academic disciplines, 11 percent. The distribution of these disciplinary areas varied widely by country (Table 3.1). While it is most likely that some students with an interest in certain disciplinary areas are attracted to specific countries for specific types of training (often at the more advanced levels), other factors are also involved, especially when an overall international picture is sought. As will be noted below, the motivation for seeking specific degrees, credentials, or subjects seems to be a primary factor in terms of international educational exchange, followed closely by foreign language study.

The question of the origin of the foreign students who were the subject of this international investigation is necessarily a complex one. Each respondent was asked to name the country of which he was a citizen as well as the one in which he was born. In an international population, the above two questions do not necessarily elicit identical information. For example, one respondent was an Asian male, born in Vietnam when it was under French control, to a Chinese mother who held a French passport, and who therefore himself held a French passport. He had grown up in Hong Kong, where he had received his undergraduate and graduate education, and he spoke Chinese and English, not French. The variety of

TABLE 3.1

Demographic Sample Statistics

(Usable respondents)	Brazil (149)	Canada (620)	France (96)	Hong Kong (42)	India (56)	Iran (73)	Japan (30)	Kenya (84)	U.K. (370)	U.S. (955)	W. Germany (42)
Sex:											
Percent male	71.8	70.2	68.8	52.4	81.8	71.2	66.7	76.2	65.7	78.6	54.0
Percent female	28.2	29.8	31.3	47.6	18.2	28.8	33.3	23.8	34.3	21.4	46.0
Age:											
Range	16–40	17–71	18–50	18–47	18–28	18–36	19–54	20–34	18–58	18–54	18–38
Mean	23.5	24.8	25.3	26.3	22.9	24.2	27.0	23.3	24.9	26.7	24.7
Mode	20	20	21	20	21	23	26	22	20	25	20
Prior residence:											
Percent urban	88.7	83.2	87.5	90.5	66.7	90.4	82.1	25.6	84.7	86.6	75.0
Percent rural	11.3	16.8	12.5	9.5	33.3	9.6	17.9	74.0	15.3	13.4	25.0
Length of time in the sojourn country (in percentages):											
Less than 1 month	.7	0.0	1.0	0.0	0.0	0.0	0.0	0.0	0.0	.1	2.4
1 to 4 months	8.8	.5	22.9	45.2	7.3	2.8	0.0	1.2	1.9	3.9	11.9
5 to 8 months	31.8	17.6	24.0	7.1	18.2	19.7	0.0	51.2	25.9	19.2	23.8
9 to 12 months	2.0	3.2	7.3	4.8	7.3	11.3	3.4	0.0	23.8	5.0	2.4
13 to 18 months	19.6	15.2	12.5	9.5	5.5	9.9	3.4	35.7	5.7	17.2	14.3
19 to 24 months	4.7	12.3	5.2	2.4	9.1	14.1	17.2	4.8	12.2	7.5	7.1
More than 2 years	32.4	51.1	27.1	31.0	52.7	42.3	75.9	7.1	30.5	47.1	38.1
Previous formal post-secondary education (in years):											
Mean	2.7	3.4	3.8	4.6	2.1	2.6	3.7	2.4	3.8	4.5	3.6
Mode	2	1	6	6	1	1	1	3	6	6	6
Academic discipline (in percentages):											
Behavioral/social sciences	13.8	17.5	18.0	43.2	18.2	10.3	19.2	11.1	24.7	22.4	14.3
Life/biological sciences	35.8	21.4	7.9	2.7	10.9	16.2	3.8	19.8	17.0	10.1	11.9
Engineering/physical sciences	31.7	31.2	30.3	10.8	18.2	14.7	34.6	24.7	25.6	47.3	7.1
Arts/humanities	8.9	16.1	34.8	29.7	29.1	16.2	26.9	12.3	25.6	12.4	66.7
Others	9.8	13.8	9.0	13.5	23.6	42.6	15.3	32.1	7.2	6.8	0.0

Source: Compiled by the authors.

combinations possible is truly astounding. Nevertheless, for purposes of analysis, it was important to have some indication of origin.

The respondents' countries of citizenship are listed in Appendix A for the total study population, and in Appendix B for the samples from each country.

For the purposes of analysis within this investigation, however, we utilized only those respondents whose countries of citizenship and birth were the same. Obviously, a listing of this sort would be too long and have too few respondents for individual countries to permit meaningful analyses and interpretation of data. Thus, geographical area divisions were formed from the data (Appendix C gives the complete listing) as follows:

Area of Origin	Number of Cases
Western Europe	198
United Kingdom	63
Eastern Europe	30
Black Africa	219
Arabic speaking	204
Iran	99
South Pacific Countries	34
South Asia	167
South East Asia	165
Other Asian Countries	291
Latin America	320
Canada	48
United States	220

Various groups were tried out before these divisions were accepted. Although the groups are by no means completely satisfactory for all purposes and some problems certainly remained, the classification adopted seems logical and workable for our purposes.

To illustrate the decisions involved in grouping data of this kind, one might at first argue that students with origins in the United States and Canada could be grouped together under the category of "North American Countries." A closer look, however, will reveal that the response patterns of the Canadians and the Americans in the international study population were distinctly different and hence they could not be grouped together without considerable cost to the interpretation of the available data. For these reasons, while most of the groupings represent geographical areas, the United Kingdom, Iran, Canada, and the United States are analyzed separately as individual countries.

It was initially planned to make a separate analysis of those students whose countries of origin and places of study were the same. Unfortunately, sufficient numbers of such respondents were not found in the sample populations. This fact is shown in Table 3.2. Consequently, the analyses within this investigation are presented in terms of the geographical area groupings listed above and categorized under the general term of "origin."

To continue with the major characteristics of foreign student populations, the respondents in all of the country samples were more likely not to have previously visited the sojourn country for more than one month prior to their present sojourn. On the other hand, in Brazil, Canada, France, Hong Kong, and Iran, the respondents were more likely to have previously visited other foreign countries for continuous periods of more than one month. (See Table 3.3.) It was hypothesized that a period of previous adjustment to a foreign culture would significantly influence the coping and adaptation process and patterns on the ground that those who had experienced a previous adjustment to a foreign culture would be more aware of what to expect and should consequently be better and more quickly able (with fewer difficulties and becoming more deeply involved in the foreign culture more quickly) to adapt during the transition into the new culture. It was thought that this might be so because these respondents would already have developed coping mechanisms relevant to the transition into a foreign culture as a result of their previous experience.

The question as to how long a student would need to have been in a foreign culture to permit the coping and adjustment processes to have begun is not one that has been previously studied. Certainly, one would not anticipate that those who had been on a quick tour of a few days in a variety of countries could be expected to have begun a personal adjustment to a foreign culture. They would, more than likely, have been exposed only to parts of a differing culture or cultures as an observer. Some evidence, although secondary, points to the conclusion that American undergraduate students do begin their adjustment to a foreign culture within a month's sojourn under certain circumstances,[1] but that would not assure that the same period of time would accomplish the same result in the case of those with origins in other parts of the world. Nevertheless, after a great deal of discussion on this matter, it was arbitrarily decided to include two items with regard to a prior visit for a continuous period of <u>one month or more</u>.

The variable was further refined by combining responses to permit a comparison between those who had "traveled" somewhere outside their home country for continuous periods of more than one month with those "untraveled": those who had not traveled for

TABLE 3.2

Participating Country Respondents at Study Sites

Studying in:	Country from which Respondents Came:											
	Brazil	Canada	France	Hong Kong	India	Iran	Japan	Kenya	U.K.	U.S.	W. Germany	Total
Brazil	—	0	0	0	0	0	1	0	0	0	0	1
Canada	12	—	21	75	16	18	6	3	18	89	7	265
France	5	3	—	0	3	2	2	0	2	4	3	24
Hong Kong	0	1	0	—	0	0	3	0	2	18	1	25
India	0	0	0	0	—	0	0	3	0	0	1	4
Iran	0	0	0	0	1	—	1	0	1	4	1	8
Japan	0	0	0	2	0	0	—	0	0	2	0	4
Kenya	0	0	0	0	0	0	2	—	1	7	0	10
U.K.	7	10	3	7	5	9	8	7	—	80	15	151
U.S.	11	34	17	29	70	70	37	1	37	—	13	319
W. Germany	0	0	6	0	0	0	0	0	2	16	—	24
Total	35	48	47	113	95	99	60	14	63	220	41	835

Source: Compiled by the authors.

TABLE 3.3

Previous Travel
(in percentages)

	Brazil	Canada	France	Hong Kong	India	Iran	Japan	Kenya	U.K.	U.S.	W. Germany
Have you previously visited the sojourn country for more than one month before your present stay?											
Yes	18.8	11.6	33.3	9.5	16.4	18.1	33.3	25.0	25.4	21.7	40.0
No	81.2	88.4	66.7	90.5	83.3	81.9	66.7	75.0	74.6	78.3	60.0
Have you visited any other foreign countries for continuous periods of more than one month?											
Yes	57.7	56.0	56.8	52.4	21.4	56.2	30.0	34.5	44.2	40.6	42.5
No	42.3	44.0	43.2	47.6	78.6	42.5	70.0	65.5	55.8	59.4	57.7
Respondents who had traveled for continuous periods of more than one month in sojourn country or in other foreign countries:											
Traveled*	63.8	58.3	65.6	52.4	33.9	61.6	50.0	42.9	52.7	49.9	69.2
Untraveled*	36.2	41.7	35.4	47.6	66.1	38.4	50.0	57.1	47.3	50.1	30.8

*Figures here represent a created category to compare only those who answered "no" on both of the above two items with those who answered "yes" on either or both items.

Source: Compiled by the authors.

continuous periods of more than one month in the sojourn country nor in other foreign countries (Table 3.3). This variable produced a more evenly distributed grouping of "traveled" and "untraveled" respondents for each country sample, and is the variable that is used throughout the analyses of these international data.

As will become clear below, this created variable is an important one, in respect to many of the international analyses as well as the individual country analyses. Further studies, however, are necessary before the period of "one month" can be accepted as the dividing line most crucial to the variable. Such studies will have to be carried out by future scholars. Even though such studies do appear to be significant factors as far as the present interviews and present statistical data are concerned, the present analysis does not consider it carefully enough.

Another important factor is the information received by the foreign student with regard to study opportunities and conditions in the sojourn country prior to leaving home. In general, the respondents in this investigation felt that the material they had was adequate (see Table 3.4). There were, however, indications that the information received in Japan, Iran, and France was incomplete and that such information could be more easily available from Hong Kong and Iran. As for the information obtainable since arriving at the host institution, this also was in general considered accessible and adequate. The adequacy of the information was, however, questioned in Japan and in France; 48.3 percent of those studying in Japan reported the information inadequate, as did 45.3 percent of those in France. A higher percentage of the sample in Iran (15.5 percent) than in the other country indicated that they had not been able to obtain the information that they needed.

Certainly, the foreign students' perception of the available information necessary for studies in the foreign institution is an important factor requiring careful consideration and, in certain countries at least, more attention. It is difficult to see how information that is perceived as inadequate or is not comprehended could possibly do anything but create difficulties in the pursuit of studies.

For the total study population, 62 percent of the respondents reported that they had made use of university publications. Of those that had used the publications, 13 percent believed that these publications had been unsatisfactory; 49 percent found them satisfactory. In general, most respondents indicated that whether or not they themselves had actually utilized such publications, they did believe that they were satisfactory. Among the respondents in Kenya, however, 25.6 percent of those using the publications reported that they had found them unsatisfactory. This was an especially high percentage in comparison with other country samples. An additional

TABLE 3.4

Perception of Information
(in percentages)

	Brazil	Canada	France	Hong Kong	India	Iran	Japan	Kenya	U.K.	U.S.	W. Germany
Before leaving your home country, did you receive enough information about study opportunities and conditions in this country?											
Yes, I was adequately informed	22.5	21.2	29.2	17.5	30.9	13.7	13.8	26.6	36.4	30.2	25.0
Yes, I was fairly well informed	27.6	45.5	25.0	32.5	29.1	32.9	37.9	36.9	40.8	43.7	50.0
No, I was not adequately informed	21.7	26.6	36.5	25.0	29.1	35.6	37.9	28.1	20.1	21.8	20.0
I had no information at all	8.2	6.6	9.4	25.0	10.9	17.8	10.3	2.4	2.7	4.4	5.0
Since arriving in this country, have you been able to obtain the information you needed for your university studies?											
Yes, and the information is quite adequate	56.8	76.3	48.4	67.5	62.5	47.9	44.8	86.9	79.2	74.5	65.0
Yes, but the information is not adequate	39.2	21.9	45.3	25.0	28.6	37.0	48.3	10.7	19.7	22.9	35.0
No, I have not been able to obtain the information I need	4.1	1.8	6.3	7.5	8.9	15.1	6.9	2.4	1.0	2.5	

Source: Compiled by the authors.

3.8 percent of the Kenya sample (nonusers) felt that the publications would probably not be satisfactory.

Most of the respondents received money from their families to finance their foreign studies. Scholarships were held by 44 percent of the population in this investigation and were especially likely to be held by those in Iran, Kenya, and France. Those in Hong Kong and the United States were more likely to have applications for scholarships "in process" at the time of this investigation (the instruments were completed at the middle of the academic year). Most of the scholarships held were provided by governments or governmental agencies, either in the host or the native country, rather than by educational institutions or other sources.

Even though most of the respondents were single, most of them did live with someone. Those who were married were more likely to be studying in the United States, Japan, Brazil, the United Kingdom, and Canada. Neither loneliness nor homesickness was reported with much frequency, especially among those who were married and had spouses present in the sojourn country.

PERCEPTIONS

In terms of motivation for journeying to a particular foreign country for study, of the total population 33.7 percent indicated that obtaining a degree or diploma from that country was a very important academic reason (71.3 percent said either "very important" or "important"). In fact, the single most important academic reason for attending a foreign university was to acquire a diploma or degree from that particular country in the case of respondents in Canada, India, Iran, Kenya, the United Kingdom, the United States, and Brazil. The single most important academic reason for journeying to France, Hong Kong, Japan, and the Federal Republic of Germany, however, was to gain knowledge of that particular country's language. On this point, respondents viewed their ability to function in the language of instruction in the particular sojourn country as satisfactory in terms of reading speed, reading comprehension, speaking in class, understanding discussions, and understanding lectures. Their ability with regard to writing papers was generally rated as quite satisfactory in all countries, although less so in Brazil.

Respondents in all countries ranked the acquisition of experience in a foreign country as the single most important social and cultural reason for going to a foreign university.

Library facilities at the sojourn institutions were regularly judged to be suited to the respondents' needs and were easy to use with the exception of those in Kenya, where 72.3 percent of the respondents felt that the facilities were suited to their needs but difficult to use. This was also the case for 28.4 percent of the respondents in France and for 23.3 percent of the respondents in Japan. The library facilities were judged as not suited to the respondents' needs by 36.6 percent of the respondents in Hong Kong.

Laboratories and other facilities at the sojourn institutions were typically judged as suited to the respondents' needs and easy to use. The single exception to this was the facilities in Kenya which were found to be suitable but difficult to use.

Advisory services specifically designed for foreign students had been used by 42 percent of the respondents. Only 13 percent of these users judged the services as unsatisfactory. An additional 33 percent of the respondents admitted that while they themselves had not used these advisory services they believed that they were satisfactory. Those who reported that the advisory services for foreign students had been used and found satisfactory were most likely to be studying in the Federal Republic of Germany, the United States, Japan, and India.

On the other hand, university counseling services at the sojourn institutions were reported to have been used by 25 percent of the respondents; 9 percent of the users assessed them to have been unsatisfactory. An additional 42 percent of the respondents indicated that while they had not used the university counseling services themselves, they did believe that they would be found to be satisfactory. The university counseling services in the Federal Republic of Germany, Brazil, and the United States were held to be the most satisfactory in users' perceptions. Those perceived as the least satisfactory by users were in Hong Kong, Kenya, and France. It should also be mentioned that while few respondents had used the services in Kenya, 69.9 percent of the sample in Kenya indicated that they believed the services would be found to be satisfactory. This was an exceptionally high figure.

Regardless of expectations and the realities encountered at the host institutions within the 11 countries, it is important to look carefully at the students' perceptions of the academic and nonacademic aspects of their experiences. The modal length of time that the respondents had been studying in the respective countries was more than 2 years with the exception of Hong Kong and Kenya, where the mode was 5 to 8 months. The individuals ranged in age from 16 to 71 years. While the judgments reported will be discussed throughout the succeeding chapters, based on the data and the case study materials, it is appropriate to begin the discussion here. Again, it is important to recall that the data were collected at the middle of the academic year. It is, of course, impossible to know whether or

TABLE 3.5

Respondents' Assessment of the Sojourn

	Brazil	Canada	France	Hong Kong	India	Iran	Japan	Kenya	U.K.	U.S.	West Germany

Part I

In general, are you satisfied with your overall ACADEMIC experience at this university thus far?

	Brazil	Canada	France	Hong Kong	India	Iran	Japan	Kenya	U.K.	U.S.	West Germany
Very satisfied	28.6%	19.0%	10.5%	9.8%	7.1%	9.7%	13.8%	25.0%	27.2%	21.0%	22.5%
Satisfied	56.5%	56.1%	51.6%	43.9%	60.7%	51.4%	41.4%	71.4%	50.4%	55.6%	52.5%
Neutral	11.6%	13.9%	16.8%	17.1%	21.4%	22.2%	31.0%	2.4%	15.5%	16.2%	15.0%
Dissatisfied	3.4%	9.2%	20.1%	22.0%	7.1%	13.9%	13.8%	1.2%	6.3%	5.9%	10.0%
Very dissatisfied	0.0%	1.8%	1.1%	7.3%	3.6%	2.8%	0.0%	0.0%	0.5%	1.3%	0.0%
Mean	1.898	2.188	2.495	2.732	2.393	2.486	2.448	1.798	2.025	2.109	2.125

In general, are you satisfied with your overall GENERAL and SOCIAL (nonacademic) experience at this university thus far?

	Brazil	Canada	France	Hong Kong	India	Iran	Japan	Kenya	U.K.	U.S.	West Germany
Very satisfied	24.3%	13.3%	5.3%	8.3%	8.9%	5.6%	10.3%	22.9%	23.1%	15.7%	12.2%
Satisfied	52.0%	42.5%	45.3%	36.1%	42.9%	36.1%	48.3%	65.1%	44.8%	44.4%	61.0%
Neutral	15.5%	24.7%	25.3%	33.3%	25.0%	34.7%	27.6%	10.8%	21.7%	26.9%	17.1%
Dissatisfied	8.1%	16.1%	16.8%	16.7%	21.4%	18.1%	13.8%	1.2%	8.7%	11.0%	9.8%
Very dissatisfied	0.0%	3.4%	7.4%	5.6%	1.8%	5.6%	0.0%	0.0%	1.6%	2.0%	0.0%
Mean	2.074	2.537	2.758	2.750	2.643	2.819	2.448	1.904	2.209	2.393	2.244

Part II

In general, how do you feel about your overall experience in this country with regard to the following two areas:

1. With general regard to my studies, I feel:

Very satisfied	28.1%	23.9%	19.1%	16.7%	33.9%	19.4%	10.0%	56.0%	29.5%	28.1%	27.0%
Satisfied	56.8%	60.2%	50.0%	38.1%	55.4%	55.6%	50.0%	42.9%	52.5%	56.8%	54.1%
Neutral	8.9%	8.8%	14.9%	26.2%	3.6%	9.7%	30.0%	1.2%	12.3%	10.2%	10.8%
Dissatisfied	6.2%	5.4%	13.8%	16.7%	5.4%	13.9%	10.0%	0.0%	5.2%	4.4%	5.4%
Very dissatisfied	0.0%	1.8%	2.1%	2.4%	1.8%	1.4%	0.0%	0.0%	0.5%	0.5%	2.7%
Mean	1.932	2.010	2.298	2.500	1.857	2.222	2.400	1.476	1.948	1.926	2.027

2. With general regard to other aspects of my experience abroad, I feel:

Very satisfied	26.1%	21.5%	16.0%	42.9%	14.3%	7.0%	20.0%	38.1%	37.8%	24.4%	25.7%
Satisfied	59.2%	53.7%	51.1%	40.5%	53.6%	39.4%	60.0%	48.8%	46.8%	52.6%	57.1%
Neutral	9.2%	16.3%	12.8%	9.5%	16.1%	39.4%	20.0%	13.1%	10.4%	16.6%	8.6%
Dissatisfied	5.6%	7.8%	12.8%	7.1%	7.1%	7.0%	0.0%	0.0%	3.8%	6.2%	8.6%
Very dissatisfied	0.0%	0.7%	7.4%	0.0%	8.9%	7.0%	0.0%	0.0%	1.1%	0.6%	0.0%
Mean	1.944	2.124	2.447	1.810	2.429	2.676	2.000	1.750	1.836	2.061	2.000

Source: Compiled by the authors.

not the respondents will or will not eventually obtain the degrees and credentials that they came for even though it seems that diplomas and graduations are generally the case.

With regard to the academic experience, the respondents generally agreed that what had been found at the sojourn institutions was generally satisfactory, and it was found very satisfactory by those studying in Kenya (Table 3.5, Part II). Respondents were also generally satisfied with regard to other aspects (nonacademic) of their sojourn experience in the countries in question. It should be noted, however, that while in general respondents were slightly more pleased with the academic rather than the nonacademic aspects of their sojourn in Brazil, Canada, France, India, Iran, Kenya, and the United States, in the case of the Federal Republic of Germany, Hong Kong, Japan, and the United Kingdom the reverse was evident to a slight degree.

The items from which these data were derived were placed as the final two items on the instrument. Similar judgments as to the respondents' satisfaction were evident on two nearly identical items placed in the middle of the instrument (Table 3.5, Part I). In the case of these items, respondents in all of the country samples were more likely to be slightly more satisfied with the academic than the nonacademic aspects of their sojourns, except in the sample from Japan where both means were identical. Interestingly enough, while a check list of problems immediately preceded the items placed in the middle of the questionnaire (Table 3.5, Part I), the bulk of the material between the two sets of items focused on contact and relations with native and non-native people, on behavioral indicators of involvement with native people, on opinions and judgments concerning them, on discrimination perceived and experienced, and on an overall evaluation of the influence on the respondent of the study experience. In most cases, little difference between the two sets of items was observable. Where they do occur they can best be explained by their position in the questionnaire.

In this chapter, we have looked at some of the perceptions of the foreign students in our investigation and we have looked at some of the characteristics of our samples. We now turn to an analysis of some of the detailed variables that are important if we are to understand coping and adaptation internationally.

NOTE

1. W. Frank Hull IV, Walter H. Lemke, Jr., and Richard T. K. Houang, The American Undergraduate, Off-Campus and Overseas: A Study of the Educational Validity of Such Programs (New York: Council on International Educational Exchange, 1977).

4

PROBLEMS AND DIFFICULTIES

In an earlier report which represented the first stage of the research conducted under the auspices of the International Committee for the Study of Educational Exchange, [1] an attempt was made to identify the major problems and difficulties faced by those attending a foreign university. The issues which were raised in this connection emerged in part from the existing literature, but they were also brought to our attention by colleagues from the seven countries which participated in this investigation. In some cases, their comments were based on interviews with samples of students, but more frequently the problems and difficulties mentioned represented judgments of the investigators themselves, frequently after consultation with those professors or foreign student advisors whose extensive personal experience made them especially knowledgeable in this regard. In the present study, students themselves told us about their problems and allowed us, as will be evident below, to discover which of these were most likely to cause concern. As an introduction to the more quantitative approach represented by these new data, we would like to present in summary form the major problems and difficulties that were discussed in the first study. It should be pointed out, however, that we were also interested on that occasion in the administrative aspects of the foreign sojourn, and that in some cases the problems that were raised concerned those responsible for the exchange programs more than those who participated in them.

This is true, for example, of the first problem raised in what might be described as a chronological or case-history approach to the exchange process, namely, the issue of selection of students for study abroad. It is our impression, shared by a number of our colleagues, that with the possible exception of certain organized programs such as some Junior Year Abroad programs, the selection

process is frequently haphazard. A number of years ago it was es-
timated that about one-third of those who went abroad were carefully screened, one-third only partially so, and one-third not
screened at all with regard to their chances for satisfactory academic and personal adjustment. Even this relatively modest estimate has been challenged as being too optimistic regarding the proportion of students adequately screened, particularly as to the personal (as distinct from the academic) characteristics likely to be
associated with success abroad.

A problem experienced more directly by the students themselves refers to entrance into the foreign university and the "credits"
granted for academic work previously completed (and also how the
studies abroad will be evaluated by the home university and in the
home country when they return). This issue is complicated by the
wide variations in university curricula in various countries, as well
as in the attitudes adopted toward courses taken elsewhere. European universities are now in the process of setting up a series of
"equivalences" to facilitate the transfer of students from one university to another, but this has not yet gone far enough to solve the
problem for the majority of foreign students.

A number of difficulties arise in connection with obtaining the
information needed in the process of preparation for the foreign sojourn. Variations in the amount of information available, and ease
or difficulty in access to it, are very great, and complaints in this
connection are relatively frequent. In our first study we wrote:

> There can be no doubt as to the importance of proper
> orientation or preparation for the foreign sojourn,
> not only as regards the university, but also the total
> community (or culture) into which the student is in-
> troduced. A great deal of unhappiness might be
> eliminated if the foreign student had a clearer pic-
> ture of what was expected of him at the academic level,
> and the trauma of "cultural shock" might be reduced if
> he knew more about general norms or standards of
> behavior.[2]

Language facility may be regarded as a special case under the general heading of adequate preparation, and one which may give rise
to major difficulties.

As far as the actual work at the university is concerned, it is
clear that a number of difficulties may arise. Most serious is academic failure, in examinations in specific courses, or in not receiving the diploma or degree toward which the foreign sojourn was
directed. There are other, more specific difficulties or annoyances

which may arise, such as the lack of access to professors or instructors who might give the student the advice required; inadequate library facilities; poor laboratory equipment; unsatisfactory level of instruction (too complex or too simple); courses which lack relevance to the student's interests, and so on. Several of these difficulties are identified by the students in this study, as will be seen below, both in the statistical tables and in the interviews.

Additional possible difficulties arise in connection with the broad problem of adapting to life in the new environment. These may relate to the task of finding suitable lodgings, to financial difficulties, to experiences of prejudice and discrimination in the host population, or to lack of satisfactory contact or of the establishment of friendly relations. All of these may create serious obstacles to a satisfactory adjustment. The question of the importance of personal contacts is the subject of a special, detailed analysis in Chapter 5; the other items on this list will be discussed later in this present chapter. We would add one further item here, namely the problem of culture shock, a term denoting patterns of behavior which differ from one culture to another, which may cause misunderstanding and even conflict, and which may result in embarrassment as a consequence of failure to recognize the meaning of the "cues" to emotional and interpersonal reactions. This may affect many aspects of social life, including male-female relations, food habits and table manners, personal status, politics, national pride, and the nature and meaning of friendship.

The first study dealt also, though briefly, with problems that may arise on the return home. This refers not only to the so-called "brain drain," which has been widely discussed, and in connection with which a report of an extensive investigation was published a few years ago.[3] When students do return, they may be faced with the problem of finding a job in which the training that they have received abroad will be put to good use. Often they are obliged to content themselves with positions at a level lower than that to which they feel entitled.[4] Sometimes study abroad means added prestige on the return home, but it may occasionally be followed by a certain degree of hostility against someone who has become a "foreigner." Our own study has not added any significant information on this important topic, although our long-term interviews 10 to 15 years after the foreign experience do yield some additional insight.

These are some of the problems and difficulties that may have to be faced by those—primarily students, but often also those at a more senior level—who spend some time at a foreign university, and as a consequence in a foreign culture. We turn now to what our data reveal regarding the difficulties seen by our respondents to have, or to have had, a negative impact on their foreign sojourn. Usually, such difficulties are surmounted sooner or later, but they can be very painful while they last. Below (Chapter 13) we shall raise the question as to how, and to what extent, steps can be taken to reduce if not to eliminate such difficulties, and thereby increase the pleasure and satisfaction of attending a foreign university. Our present task is to report on the difficulties encountered.

DIFFICULTIES REPORTED BY FOREIGN STUDENTS

In the present study, foreign students studying at universities in 11 countries were asked to indicate on a check list the difficulties that they had encountered. Table 4.1 shows the percentage of students, listed by country, who specified a particular problem or source of difficulty.

We are immediately struck by three results, namely (1) the large number of different difficulties encountered, (2) the substantial proportions of students who have had to face them during the course of their foreign sojourn, and (3) the large variations from country to country. (We should add, however, that our analysis of the course of the sojourn on the basis of three different interviews with students at the beginning, the middle, and the end of the year, shows that many of the difficulties are indeed surmounted before the year is over.)

The figures presented in Table 4.1 give the results in detail, but it seems to us worth while to draw attention to some of the specific findings. We shall look first at the difficulties which relate more directly to the university itself, and then at those that are concerned with adaptation to the society or culture as a whole, although in some instances the line of demarcation may be difficult to establish. In the present context, we have arbitrarily used a cutoff point of 10 percent; if fewer than that proportion specify a particular difficulty, we have considered it relatively unimportant, although in the case of specific individuals it may indeed represent a serious problem.

Among the difficulties mentioned in the introductory portion of this chapter, one to which our earlier study attributed great importance, was facility in the local language. This is a difficulty related both to the university and the society as a whole, but is undoubtedly felt most acutely in the former context. In the present study, it ranges in frequency from a low of 12.3 percent in Iran, 13.8 percent in the United Kingdom, and 14.3 percent in the United States, to highs of 40.5 percent in Hong Kong and 42.9 percent in Kenya. The problem does not appear to be as serious in Japan (16.7 percent) as our earlier study indicated, but we must add that the majority of the students had been there more than two years.

The complaint of "lack of framework and direction in the academic program" is found most frequently in France (35.4 percent), which fits with the common perception of the inaccessibility of the French teaching staff, and the difficulty of obtaining academic guidance; the percentage drops to 9.5 percent in Kenya. On the other hand, "lack of personal counseling," which may refer to help needed in connection with personal rather than academic difficulties, is found most frequently in Brazil (26.8 percent), and drops below 10 percent in Hong Kong and the United Kingdom. The accessibility of tutors in many British colleges and universities and in those patterned on the British model may explain this finding. The relatively low figure in American and German universities for this item (below 11 percent) may be due to the availability of foreign student advisors or others filling a similar role.

The "problem of equivalence or proper placement level on arrival" is most serious in Kenya (32.1 percent) and goes down below 10 percent in Hong Kong, the United States, and the United Kingdom. This issue, as indicated above, appears serious enough in most countries to deserve more attention than it has so far received: somewhat less serious, apparently, is the feeling of "insufficient previous training," in connection with which only in Brazil (20.8 percent) does it assume substantial proportions. This is probably because the particular university in which the data were obtained has a reputation for relatively high standards as compared with other Latin American universities from which most of the foreign students came. "Difficulties in dealing with the university administration" are much more frequent in India (37.5 percent) than anywhere else, and it is also in India that we find most frequent complaints (32.1 percent) as to "lack of information regarding progress in studies"; this is very rarely mentioned in the United States. "Difficulty of courses" and "problems with examinations" are both more common in Brazil than elsewhere, probably for the reason mentioned above.

Related more directly to housing, but relevant to the work at the university, is the complaint about "lack of a private place to study," checked by 35.7 percent in Kenya and 32.1 percent in India. This problem appears to have been solved in West Germany (2.4 percent), at least at the particular university where the German sample was obtained.

The question of contact, both with fellow students at the university and with the local population in general, is the subject of detailed analysis in Chapter 5, and only a brief statement in that regard will be made at this point. The problem of "lack of contact with fellow students" is recognized most frequently by foreign students

TABLE 4.1

Problems and Sources of Difficulties: Percent of Country Samples Specifying Difficulties

Item	Brazil	Canada	France	Hong Kong	India	Iran	Japan	Kenya	U.K.	U.S.	West Germany
Financial problems	34.9	23.5	34.4	16.7	37.5	26.0	23.3	66.7	19.5	28.0	19.0
Ill health	16.1	7.9	15.6	16.7	30.4	9.6	16.7	13.1	8.9	6.9	14.3
Personal depression	32.2	24.5	21.9	21.4	30.4	15.1	6.7	16.7	20.8	19.4	11.9
Difficulty adjusting to climate	25.5	21.9	26.0	23.8	53.8	12.3	0.0	19.0	21.6	17.4	21.4
Difficulty adjusting to local food	25.5	11.8	12.5	9.5	51.8	24.7	3.3	21.4	14.6	16.9	19.0
Difficulty with the local language	25.5	22.7	16.7	40.5	32.1	12.3	16.7	42.9	13.8	16.9	14.3
Lack of opportunity to use the local language	9.4	18.5	21.9	9.5	23.2	4.1	16.7	39.3	4.9	12.4	14.3
Relations with the opposite sex	10.7	17.4	24.0	21.4	35.7	21.9	10.0	46.4	12.4	14.0	4.8
Problems relating to religion	4.7	4.7	2.1	2.4	12.5	4.1	3.3	7.1	5.4	4.1	7.1
Lack of framework and direction in academic program	16.8	18.1	35.4	16.7	26.8	24.7	20.0	9.5	19.7	13.5	19.0
Lack of personal counseling	26.8	16.8	16.7	2.4	23.2	24.7	20.0	31.0	8.4	10.9	11.9
Lack of contact with fellow students	20.1	19.0	32.3	19.0	19.6	15.1	23.3	7.1	14.9	15.6	4.8

	1	2	3	4	5	6	7	8	9	10	11
Lack of contact with local people	18.1	31.1	47.9	14.3	26.8	13.7	13.3	15.5	24.1	24.2	11.9
Lack of motivation in my studies	20.8	17.7	14.6	28.6	25.0	16.4	20.0	8.3	15.7	12.1	9.5
Lack of facilities for recreation and sports	28.9	10.5	26.0	16.7	39.3	32.9	16.7	19.0	10.8	7.5	11.9
Lack of a private place to study	26.8	9.7	9.4	19.0	32.1	23.3	13.3	35.7	8.4	13.1	2.4
Problems with examinations	22.1	13.2	12.5	7.1	21.4	13.7	16.7	10.7	9.2	15.0	11.9
Difficulty of courses	24.8	15.5	8.3	4.8	8.9	5.5	16.7	10.7	9.5	10.9	4.8
Lack of information regarding progress in studies	16.8	13.9	18.8	16.7	32.1	23.3	23.3	26.2	16.2	7.1	11.9
Difficulties in dealing with the university administration	17.4	11.6	18.8	11.9	37.5	20.5	10.0	15.5	5.1	9.9	9.5
Insufficient previous training	20.8	12.7	9.4	2.4	16.1	8.2	10.0	7.1	8.9	8.8	11.9
Problems of equivalence or proper placement level upon arrival	18.1	11.8	12.5	9.5	12.5	15.5	10.0	32.1	5.4	6.0	19.0
A change in your objectives	8.1	10.3	7.3	2.4	10.7	8.2	3.3	1.2	6.5	6.0	4.8
Other	2.0	6.5	8.3	11.9	3.6	1.4	--	1.2	5.7	4.0	4.8

Source: Compiled by the authors.

in France (32.3 percent), but remains fairly important everywhere
else, with the exception of Kenya and West Germany. As for "lack
of contact with local people," once again it is the foreign students in
France who complain about this to a striking degree (47.9 percent),
with a relatively high percentage also in Canada (31.1 percent), and
with more than 10 percent everywhere else.

This issue of contact leads us into the difficulties reported with
regard to the culture or society as a whole. "Relations with the opposite sex" might be expected to cause some trouble; they do particularly in Kenya (46.4 percent) and India (35.7 percent), substantially in most other countries, and are almost never mentioned in
West Germany (4.8 percent). "Difficulty in adjusting to climate"
and also to local food is particularly common in India (more than 50
percent in both cases), and are indicated with some frequency in
most other countries. Difficulties relating to finances are reported
with great frequency, reaching 66.7 percent in Kenya, and remaining above 15 percent in all samples. Problems regarding religion
are practically nonexistent, reaching the 10 percent level only in
India (12.5 percent). (The issue of housing, which often creates
very serious difficulties for foreign students, is dealt with in detail
below.)

Another way of looking at problems and difficulties is to discover which among them are regarded as most troublesome. Table
4.2 indicates for each country the five areas which in the students'
judgment gave them the most difficulty; these are ranked from first
to fifth in importance.

This presentation adds another dimension to the present analysis, since it is possible for a difficulty to arise frequently, and yet
not be considered especially troublesome. This is the case, apparently, with "lack of personal counseling," which appears only in Japan
(third); "problems with examinations" appearing only in France
(fourth); and "lack of information regarding progress in studies,"
which appears only in Hong Kong (third). "Difficulty in adjusting to
local food" is ranked first in India and third in the United States.
Most striking is the fact that "lack of contact with local people" is
mentioned less frequently as a difficulty in West Germany than anywhere else (only 11.9 percent), yet appears as the most troublesome
item in that country, ranking first in that respect. The inference
which we draw from these findings is that an estimate of the importance of any single item should take into account both its frequency
and its ranking on a scale of troublesomeness.

Among the items which are most frequently mentioned as caus-
ing the greatest trouble, the one concerning "financial problems" is
outstanding. They are ranked first in all countries except two, namely India (second) and Kenya (third). No other item approaches this in

importance. "Relations with the opposite sex" appears in six countries, "personal depression" in five, "adjustment to climate" and "lack of contact with local people" in four. "Problems of equivalence" in placement within the university is mentioned among the most troublesome in only three countries, but ranks highest in West Germany (together with lack of contact), and second in Kenya.

One additional comment should be made regarding financial difficulties: they clearly create serious problems in the judgment of a substantial proportion of foreign students. Many of them come to a foreign university with fellowships, and in their case (as our interviews demonstrate), the major complaint is that the monthly or quarterly stipends do not arrive on time. Although it may be difficult to persuade governments or foundations to increase the size of their fellowships, it should not be so difficult to reduce if not to eliminate the delay in transmitting the promised funds. Those students who come without fellowships may be supported by their families, and in their case, complaints are relatively rare; but others who come on their own hoping to earn money abroad are frequently frustrated by local regulations forbidding remunerative employment. Some succeed in working in a clandestine manner (what the French call "le travail au noir") without working papers which, as students, they find it impossible to obtain. This problem can only be solved, in our judgment, through some sort of international agreement which will take into consideration the special needs of students, but as far as we know there have been no steps taken so far in this direction.

The question of housing came up indirectly in connection with the item "lack of a private place to study"; it is of course directly related to the problem of finances, but it seemed to us to be of sufficient importance to warrant a specific analysis. In our earlier study we pointed out that

> the question of lodgings for foreign students has
> aroused considerable interest on the part of our col-
> leagues in this study. . . . There is a general feel-
> ing that not enough lodging is available at prices within
> the range of the foreign students' income, and the dif-
> ficulties which arise as a consequence represent one
> of the major sources of the complaints heard. As for
> the kind of lodging to be recommended, no clear con-
> sensus emerges; perhaps the most reasonable conclu-
> sion is that some students are happier in dormitories,
> others like the idea of living with a local family, still
> others prefer to be by themselves. It appears to be
> impossible to make a decision in this connection which
> would hold for all foreign students. [5]

TABLE 4.2

Problems and Sources of Difficulties: Ranking by Country of the Five Most Troublesome Areas

Item	Brazil	Canada	France	Hong Kong	India	Iran	Japan	Kenya	U.K.	U.S.	West Germany
Financial problems	1	1	1	1	2	1	1	3	1	1	
Ill health					2				4	4	3
Personal depression		3	4			4			2		
Difficulty adjusting to climate	3	2			2					3	
Difficulty adjusting to local food					1					3	
Lack of opportunity to use the local language		4	4					5			
Relations with the opposite sex			2		2			5	4	5	3
Lack of framework and direction in academic program				3			1				3
Lack of personal counseling							3				
Lack of contact with fellow students						5					3

Category				
Lack of contact with local people	5	3	4	1
Lack of motivation in my studies	3	3		
Lack of facilities for recreation and sports	3	4	2	
Lack of a private place to study		3	3	1
Problems with examinations		4		
Lack of information regarding progress in studies		3	3	
Difficulties in dealing with the university administration	3	3	2	5
Insufficient previous training	2		3	
Problems of equivalence or proper placement level upon arrival	4	3	2	1

Source: Compiled by the authors.

In the present study, we asked the students to check the problems and sources of difficulty which they encountered in connection with housing (Table 4.3).

Once again there are striking variations among the different countries. "Excessive expense of housing" varies from 44.8 percent in France and 36.7 percent in Japan to only 9.5 percent in West Germany; "lack of personal privacy" from 39.3 percent in Kenya to a low of 11.9 percent, again in West Germany. "Difficulties with local transportation" are common in India (33.9 percent) and Brazil (33.6 percent) but very rare in Kenya (4.8 percent) and Japan (3.3 percent). The "lack of general comfort and of cleanliness" is complained of more frequently in India and Kenya than anywhere else. "Lack of available housing" in general is reported in more than 25 percent of the cases in Kenya, Brazil, Japan, West Germany, and India, and exceeds 10 percent in all countries.

The students were also asked to place the difficulties and problems regarding housing in a rank order from most to least troublesome. "Excessive expense" was most pronounced, ranking highest in seven countries, second in Brazil, third in India, and lower in Kenya and West Germany. In Brazil, the most troublesome was "difficulties with local transportation" (the university where data were collected is a considerable distance from the city); in Hong Kong and West Germany it was "lack of personal privacy"; in Kenya it was "lack of general comfort," and in West Germany "lack of personal privacy" (Table 4.4).

Once again we are reminded of the difficulty of speaking of the foreign student in view of the striking variations from one country to another. It remains true, however, that there are some findings that are fairly general. Excessive expense of housing is a complaint almost everywhere, whereas distance from shopping areas, insufficient furnishings, and inadequate accommodations "for my family" are relatively rarely indicated. The issue of what is widespread and what is specific to each country will be discussed further in Chapter 11.

There are three additional sources of possible difficulty which have not so far been included in this discussion. The first source, which can be a source of great unhappiness in many cases, refers to the experience of ethnic prejudice and discrimination on the part of the host population. The second source, equally serious, relates to feelings of loneliness and homesickness. Both of these will be dealt with in Chapter 6. The third source, to which we now turn, is rather less acute in its consequences, but may affect the general satisfaction or dissatisfaction with the whole sojourn at the foreign university; it refers to the judgment regarding the teaching received, and to the relations with the faculty at the host institution.

TABLE 4.3

Problems and Sources of Difficulties Relating to Housing:
Percent of Country Samples Specifying Difficulties

Item	Brazil	Canada	France	Hong Kong	India	Iran	Japan	Kenya	U.K.	U.S.	West Germany
Excessive expense of housing	32.2	32.7	44.8	19.0	17.9	13.7	36.7	17.9	24.1	28.0	9.5
Lack of personal privacy	25.5	14.2	18.8	16.7	32.1	32.9	16.7	39.3	13.2	15.3	11.9
Difficulties with local transportation	33.6	6.0	15.6	9.5	33.9	28.8	3.3	4.8	10.8	20.4	19.0
Lack of available housing	26.8	10.6	21.9	11.9	25.0	19.2	26.7	41.7	18.1	18.2	26.2
Distance from the university	28.9	11.5	21.9	9.5	25.0	11.0	23.3	21.4	14.3	9.8	21.4
Distance from shopping areas	20.8	6.8	11.5	21.4	32.1	16.4	6.7	11.9	14.6	19.9	16.7
Lack of general comfort in lodging at present	22.8	16.8	26.0	9.5	39.3	31.5	10.0	35.7	11.4	12.0	16.7
Lack of cleanliness of lodging at present	10.7	10.3	11.5	19.0	42.9	21.9	0.0	39.3	14.9	7.1	2.4
Insufficient or inadequate accommodations for my family at present	8.1	3.4	2.1	0.0	5.4	8.2	6.7	1.2	3.2	3.2	4.8
Insufficient or inadequate supply of furnishings	19.5	13.2	17.7	7.1	30.4	24.7	6.7	4.8	9.7	10.5	2.4
Other	4.0	3.5	10.4	7.1	14.3	4.1	3.3	6.0	7.6	4.9	16.7

Source: Compiled by the authors.

41

TABLE 4.4

Problems and Sources of Difficulties Relating to Housing:
Ranking by Country of the Most Troublesome Areas

Item	Brazil	Canada	France	Hong Kong	India	Iran	Japan	Kenya	U.K.	U.S.	West Germany
Excessive expense of housing	2	1	1	1	3	1	1	5	1	1	5
Lack of personal privacy	4	2	2	2	1	4	3	2		2	1
Difficulties with local transportation	1		4		4	2			4	4	5
Lack of available housing	3	5	4		4	3	2	3	2	3	2
Distance from the university	5	3	3	4				5	4		5
Distance from shopping areas	5			4							2
Lack of general comfort in lodging at present		4			2	4	3	1	4		2
Lack of cleanliness of lodging at present				3			3	4	3		
Insufficient or inadequate supply of furnishings		5			4						

Source: Compiled by the authors.

Students were asked to rate a number of their experiences in this connection, the scale used ranging from "very satisfactory" (value of 1) through to "very unsatisfactory" (value of 5). This means that in Table 4.5, the higher the figure, the greater the amount of dissatisfaction reported.

Again we find considerable variation, but if we accept the figure of 3 as the line of demarcation between satisfaction and dissatisfaction, we can draw the following conclusions. Out of the 44 judgments made (11 countries times 4 items), there are only two which exceed the figure 3, one being 3.2 in the case of "accessibility of the majority of teachers" in France. This is not too surprising. A factor which played a role in the events of May ("les évènements de mai") in 1968 was the phenomenon of the "mandarinat" in France, reflecting the distance which separated professors from students. The degree of separation was reduced for a time after "the events," but was soon reestablished. The other judgment exceeding the level of 3 refers to "intellectual stimulation" provided in Iran (3.3). Other items on which the level of 3.0 was reached were "the helpfulness of teachers in general," also in Iran; "intellectual stimulation" in Hong Kong and Japan; and "teacher accessibility" in Japan and Iran. In general, therefore, we feel justified in concluding that satisfaction with the teaching staff is relatively widespread. As far as variations among countries are concerned, "teaching quality" is rated highest in Kenya (2.0) with Brazil next (2.1) and lowest in Hong Kong (2.9); "helpfulness" highest in the United Kingdom (2.0) with the United States next (2.1) and lowest in Iran (3.0); "intellectual stimulation" again highest in Kenya (2.0) and lowest in Iran (3.3); and "accessibility" highest in the United States (2.2) and lowest in France (3.2). The average ratings are below 2.5 (which means definitely satisfactory) in Brazil, Canada, Kenya, the United Kingdom, and the United States; above 2.5 but below 3.0 in France, Hong Kong, India, Japan, and West Germany; above 3 only in Iran.

It is not our purpose to establish a hierarchy of universities in the 11 countries. The samples in some cases are rather small, and the criteria we have used for ranking are limited. Our hope in this connection is that if the universities involved become aware of these findings, those who administer programs for foreign students may be willing to look into their arrangements for foreign students and ask themselves whether enough is being done to give them what they have come for.

TABLE 4.5

Experience with the Teaching Staff

In terms of your own personal experience with the teaching staff, how do you rate the following topics?	Brazil	Canada	France	Hong Kong	India	Iran	Japan	Kenya	U.K.	U.S.	West Germany
The teaching quality in general	2.1	2.3	2.5	2.9	2.5	2.5	2.7	2.0	2.3	2.2	2.4
The helpfulness of teachers in general	2.3	2.3	2.6	2.4	2.4	3.0	2.6	2.2	2.0	2.1	2.7
Intellectual stimulation provided	2.5	2.5	2.9	3.0	2.7	3.3	3.0	2.0	2.3	2.4	2.7
Accessibility of the majority of teachers	2.4	2.4	3.2	2.8	2.7	3.0	3.0	2.4	2.4	2.2	2.5

Note: The above figures represent the means responses for each country sample on a scale of "very satisfactory" (value of 1) through "very unsatisfactory" (value of 5). "No comment/not applicable" and omit responses were not used in the calculation of the means.

Source: Compiled by the authors.

THE INTERVIEWS

In Chapter 8 we shall attempt to bring together the information yielded by our case studies, particularly those in which the same foreign students were interviewed on three occasions—at the beginning, the middle, and toward the end of their year abroad. At this point, we shall limit ourselves to a brief reference to two conclusions which emerge from the interviews regarding the problems and difficulties analyzed in this chapter. The first refers to the frequency with which problems are solved before the end of the year abroad. Lodgings are often unsatisfactory at first, but some improvement is usually experienced sooner or later; depressions tend to be reduced or to disappear; language skills improve and local food becomes more palatable. Secondly, there is often a more or less philosophic acceptance of certain difficulties as being inevitable, and an accompanying refusal to allow them to spoil the total experience. This was the case with a number of foreign students in France, for example, who at first complained about the difficulty of making French friends, but who finally decided that this was inevitable, "the French are like that," and placed the accent on other aspects of their French sojourn which they found more rewarding. We are not suggesting that the problems are unimportant or that they should be ignored by those responsible for exchange programs. Obviously, the sooner they can be resolved, the better for the whole experience abroad.

THE RETROSPECTIVE STUDY

The principal results of our study of the impact of the foreign sojourn in retrospect 10 to 15 years after the experience will be presented in Chapter 7. Here we should like to report briefly on the kinds of difficulties that these more senior scholars remembered even after this considerable passage of time. (See Table 4.6.) The respondents (575 in all) are native to and presently working in the same 11 countries in which we studied foreign students. They were asked: "To what extent, if any, did you experience DIFFICULTIES during your study experience abroad in the following areas." This was followed by a list of possible areas in which difficulties might have arisen, and the respondents checked for each of them whether there were MANY, FEW, NONE, or NOT APPLICABLE.

In general, the Americans at times found difficulties with study and research facilities at the foreign institutions; the Indians were slightly bothered by time pressures; the Japanese had some difficulties with language for both academic as well as social communication

TABLE 4.6

Difficulties Recalled during the Sojourn: Rank* and Percent Response

Area	Brazil	Canada	France	Hong Kong	India	Iran	Japan	Kenya	U.K.	U.S.
Language, for academic purposes	1 12%		3 9%	3 10%			1 11%			3 10%
Language, for social purposes			1 16%	3 10%			1 11%		1 6%	3 10%
Adjustment to local customs/life style		3 7%		3 10%				3 20%	3 3%	
Loneliness	3 6%	2 9%						3 20%	3 3%	
Homesickness	2 9%	2 9%				1 28%		1 40%		
Time pressures				3 10%	1 5%	2 15%			1 6%	
Availability of information on courses, university requirements, etc.				3 10%			3 7%			
Availability of relevant information regarding local customs		1 23%		2 11%						

Availability of appropriate courses								2 11%
Study/research facilities				3 10%	2 8%		2 5%	1 16%
Availability of or access to teaching staff				2 11%				
Diet				3 10%			3 3%	
Social relations with local people	3 6%	2 9%	2 10%	3 10%	2 8%		1 6%	
Making friends				3 10%				
Housing		2 9%					2 5%	
Financial support and maintenance		2 9%	2 10%	1 30%	3 13%	2 30%	2 5%	

*Rank is based upon those respondents by country who reported "many" difficulties during their experience abroad. Only ranks 1, 2, and 3 are reported here, and only those areas are listed which were ranked 1, 2, or 3 by respondents in any single country sample.

Source: Compiled by the authors.

purposes; the Brazilians with language for social purposes and academic study as well as homesickness; those from Hong Kong and Kenya with finances; some Canadians felt the lack of information regarding local customs; and the Kenyans and Iranians were more bothered by homesickness. Those from Hong Kong remembered the greatest number of areas that had given them many difficulties. The respondents also recalled difficulties with regard to social contact with native people. Overall, however, the problems reported and their frequency of mention were not in any way excessive. For example, most of the percentage responses to particular difficulties were from less than 16 percent of the sample from each country. Only two areas had percentage responses in excess of one quarter of the individual country sample: 40 percent of the Kenyans and 28 percent of the Iranians reported difficulties with homesickness; 30 percent of both the Kenyans and those from Hong Kong with finances. Otherwise, reported difficulties ranged widely and do not lend themselves to clear generalizations.

One additional problem, not included in the list we asked our respondents to check, emerges clearly in some of our interviews, and deserves more attention than it has so far received. It is, however, indicated in the paper by one of the authors,[6] which deals with Americans who had been abroad as participants in the Senior Fulbright-Hays Program. (Their report constitutes a part of the present study.) The report takes note of the small minority of

> respondents who were most bitter in their comments were also those individuals who had been at locations where local arrangements seemed not to have been clearly formulated in advance and where advanced preparation seemed to have been poor on the part of the host institutions.[7]

This complaint is voiced by a minority, but it seems highly probable that such lack of preparation by the host university is found with considerable frequency, and that the passage of time reduces its salience. It probably occurs more frequently in some countries than in others, but our own conversations with a number of recent Fulbright appointees convince us that it may be a serious problem for many at the beginning of the foreign sojourn. One of the present authors is a member of the Franco-American Commission for Educational Exchange, and in that connection has been able to verify the frequency with which American Fellows find themselves at a loss when they first arrive. This experience is by no means limited to French universities, and in a different form affects arriving foreign students as well as more senior scholars. Unlike many other problems affecting sojourn at a foreign university, this one should be capable of solution.

NOTES

1. Otto Klineberg, International Educational Exchange (Paris: Mouton, 1976).

2. Ibid., p. 33.

3. William A. Glaser, Brain Drain and Study Abroad (New York: Columbia University, Bureau of Applied Social Research, 1974).

4. John Useem and Ruth H. Useem, The Western-Educated Man in India (New York: Dryden, 1955).

5. Klineberg, op. cit., pp. 41, 42.

6. W. Frank Hull IV and Walter H. Lemke, Jr., "Retrospective Assessment of the United States Senior Fulbright-Hays Program," International Educational and Cultural Exchange 13, no. 2 (Spring 1978): 6-9.

7. Ibid., p. 9.

5

SOCIAL CONTACT:
THE PROBLEM OF
PERSONAL INTERACTIONS
AND FRIENDSHIPS

When foreign students enter another culture, they leave behind various people, assumptions, and habits, most of which have been taken for granted for years, and enter into a new milieu filled with new people, new ways of doing things, and new assumptions about many things, including the interaction between individuals. These students realize that things will be different, but how different and in which particular ways? Often they become frustrated in the new environment and with the very people with whom dealings are imperative.

Sometimes the differences are most startling even when the host culture and the home culture might be considered somewhat similar and without a serious language barrier. For example, in the middle of an initial year in America, a woman graduate student who had journeyed to London with three teenage children and who hoped to collect materials for her thesis wrote:

> I am not terribly depressed but I find that I have become in the past few weeks, increasingly irritable at what I have chosen to identify as the "dreadful inefficiency of British people." . . . What I have found is that the charm of going to the greengrocers for one thing, the butchers for another, the bakery for a third, the iron-mongers for one kitchen utensil and the chemists for another has rather lost its charm—especially without a car—why can't I go to one place or even one shopping area to get everything? . . . I am truly tired of having to travel miles to get a complete shopping list done—nothing exotic: 1 spool of brown thread, 1 bottle of Flex shampoo, bread, mince, airmail stationery,

lightbulbs, a newspaper (not even a special one), and a keyring. That's an actual shopping list and it actually took six stores to get those things. . . .

I am quite convinced that this is what I've picked out to blame my discomfort on . . . at least I have hope that things will improve. . . . One rather great advantage of age is the recognition that nothing is permanently wonderful—all very relative. And lest you think I am disenchanted—in fact, I still love it here—it's just that the "intrigue," as one of the kids termed it, is not so intriguing anymore—it's real life, folks, and coping with it as such. . . .

My landladly plays a not insignificant part in my disenchantment—I'm so tired of hassling with her. Never in my life have I had this sort of problem with a landlady—true, I haven't had too many, but two in the past several years. I feel I've been terribly fair with her and I can't say I feel she's been likewise. This "lady," who does not want anyone to know that she "lets places," has three houses, wants her tenants to adore and respect her and has the gall to do such things as send a note to me telling me to keep my children out of the passage between our house because "we have always been very careful to protect our privacy from tenants" and at the same time is quite comfortable walking into our flat without knocking or ringing the bell (three times in the last eight days) or coming in to remove chairs ("My Dear, they're Edwardian, quite valuable, you know, you wouldn't want to be responsible, I'm sure"). In fact, those chairs were Victorian without question, and I wouldn't at all have minded being responsible. . . .

At any rate, I decided that rather than sit around and moan about it, I'd do something so Joyce (an American professor who lives in the building) and I went round on Monday night and knocked on all our neighbors' doors (those who rent from Mrs. P., who is away until mid-January), and we had a meeting at my flat to form an informal tenants association. . . .

So, I'm feeling a little more up. Christmas was nice and we had a beautiful snowfall late Monday night. The kids and I went out and had a snowball fight and built a snowman at 1:30 a.m.! It's crisp and cold and snow is still on the ground with more predicted. I love it, being an old Southerner who never had a white Christmas and hasn't seen all that much snow.

The writer described herself as "irritable," with "discomfort" and "disenchantment," but as she said, "I still love it here." Then came her decision to do something affirmative (with regard to the landlady), and "Christmas was nice and we had a beautiful snowfall." Things seemed to get better, relatively speaking. The frustrations were real ones: some aspects went against her expectations as an American living where one-stop shopping centers are everywhere and landladies have different norms of behavior.

The issue is neither her expectations nor the local conditions and assumptions, but rather the meeting of the two in a context where the unexpected, and sometimes the unacceptable, will happen.

Certainly all of this can be expected to have an influence on her academic reason for being in London, that is, the collection of materials for a thesis. What is she to do in the situation? Do we counsel her: "Oh, just wait a bit, things will get better," "Possibly you need to return home or at least take a vacation," "Just concentrate more on your academic goals for being here and remember that all of this is just temporary for you," or something else?

An alternative aspect seems appropriate: What kinds and quantities of positive, personal interactions were she and her teenage daughters having with native Londoners, who have lived all their lives with the objects and occurrences that were frustrating to her?

A MODIFIED CULTURE CONTACT HYPOTHESIS*

Based on the study made in the United States as well as the findings of others, it seemed appropriate to propose a slight

----

*This hypothesis was initially formulated in: W. Frank Hull IV, Foreign Students in the United States: Coping Behavior Within the Educational Environment (New York: Praeger, 1978), pp. 104, 105. It was subsequently discussed further at an international symposium held at the State University of New York at Buffalo and appeared under the title "A Modified Culture Contact Hypothesis and the Adaptation of Foreign Students in Cross Cultural Settings," in The Adaptation of Foreign Students in Cross-Cultural Settings, ed. Stephen P. Dunnett (State U. of N.Y. at Buffalo, Special Studies Series, Council on International Studies, 1979). Permission to adapt and publish materials from both previous sources for this section is gratefully acknowledged.

reformulation of the way experiences of transition into a foreign culture have been viewed. Termed a modified culture contact hypothesis, this argues that those foreign students who are satisfied and comfortable with their interactions with local people and the local culture during their sojourn would report broader and more general satisfaction with their total sojourn experience, not only nonacademically but also academically. Here "local people" refers to students and non-students alike, within and outside the educational community.

The argument is that contact is a complex variable that itself can generate more contact which, in turn, is generalized as positive or negative experience throughout the total sojourn. Simply put, the more contact there is with local people, the more satisfying the overall sojourn experience is likely to be.

While some factors prior to arrival will influence contact with the local people at least initially—especially prior international experience—over time it is not these factors that make the major difference in the sojourn experience. Rather, it is the experience of contact during the actual sojourn that generates more contact as well as a feeling of more general satisfaction and less dissatisfaction about various aspects of the sojourn, bringing about something like a snowball effect. A negative experience (for example, being the object of discrimination) will almost certainly influence the foreign student's reaction to the sojourn, but even such an experience may and can be countered by later positive contact with local people. While there may be a relationship between early satisfying contact, further contact, and attitudes, even initially negative contacts can be overcome given sufficient satisfying contact later on, almost, it seems, up to the point of departure. Although going well beyond our data, it may also be true that those experiencing positive contact with local people throughout their sojourn will be likely to report greater impact on their lives professionally as well as personally over the years following the sojourn.

The hypothesis is termed a "modified culture contact hypothesis" because it relates somewhat to what others have suggested but it displays major differences. Under what has been called "the association hypothesis," C. Selltiz, et al.,[1] H. Chang,[2] S. E. M. Ibrahim,[3] and A. K. Basu and Richard G. Ames,[4] have, in nearly identical ways, hypothesized that the more interaction there is between members of different cultures, the more mutually favorable attitudes will develop. "Association" refers to exposure to the foreign culture primarily through interpersonal relations but also through secondary encounters with such culture. Indeed, positive attitudes are associated with cultural contact, but the relationship goes far beyond attitudes alone.

SOCIAL CONTACT IN THE INTERNATIONAL POPULATION

The study of social contact is difficult because contact between individuals is an elusive concept that defies precise definition. This is especially so in the international sphere. What is seen as contact by one individual may be seen as nothing but pure routine politeness by another. This happens regularly between individuals and is even more extreme when cultures or subcultures are involved.

Foreign students are quick to point out that the French are superficial and unconcerned about them, but identical comments come from students in other countries as well. For some, social contact means a relationship that they assess as ordinary, even superficial. Yet whether it is seen as superficial or not depends upon the person making that judgment. Certain behaviors and points of contact are viewed as having much more significance in some cultures than in others. For example, Japanese rarely entertain guests at dinner in their homes, while this is frequently the procedure in the United States. In Ghana, a great deal of significance may be placed on sharing a drink with someone who comes to one's home. The meaning of handshakes, claps on the back, or other forms of interaction between individuals varies between cultures—indeed, it also varies within cultures.

Various questions were put to the study population under the general area of social contact, based on what others have discovered and also on the best advice that was available internationally. Some of the items worked; some did not. Nevertheless, our data yield some new insights.

To begin with, it was felt appropriate to find out if social contact was occurring between the foreign student respondents and local individuals. For this purpose it was desirable to find out more about the types of individuals with whom the foreign students were spending their time: local individuals (students, non-students, or families); fellow national students; or other foreign students. The obvious reason for such a division of categories was the huge quantity of literature and comment concerning what some have labeled "foreign student ghettos" on campus, that is, the observed behavior of foreign students sticking together in pairs or groups during their free time and also with regard to their patterns of residence in the sojourn community.

Two questions attempted to tap these areas: (1) When you are in the company of others, are they mainly . . . and (2) With which of the following groups does your present lodging bring you into regular contact? The options for both items were those listed above: local individuals (students, non-students, or families); fellow national students; other foreign students; and a final option called "others, please specify." The difficulty with such forced-choice items in this area is an obvious one: respondents are aware that in reality their relationships are too complex to be neatly and completely categorized according to the schema presented in this investigation. Thus we deal only with those respondents willing to accept the forced-choice and categorize their contact as one of the presented options. On most variables, this meant we were able to utilize about 75 percent of the original country samples.

The data based on these items are presented in Table 5.1 and indicate different situations in different country samples. Respondents who made multiple responses within any given item were deleted. Those responding "other" were also not included. As indicated above, the data analyzed and presented are only for those respondents who accepted the forced-choice nature of the items and made a single selection among the presented options with regard to their social contacts.

As is evident from the data, in certain countries more than half of the respondents reported spending their time mainly with fellow nationals or with other foreign students rather than with native people. Specifically, 67 percent of the respondents in both France and Canada reported that when they were in the company of others, the others were mainly either fellow nationals or other foreign students. This was the case also with the respondents in Hong Kong and Iran, as well as with 56 percent in the United States, 52 percent in the United Kingdom, and 51 percent in Kenya.

It also seems evident that being a foreign student in a relatively large university community, as was the situation in the Canadian sample, does not necessarily result in spending more time with native people. Conversely, it also seems evident that being a foreign student within a relatively small university community, as in Iran or Hong Kong, is not very different. Being in a university community with either a large or a small number of foreign students does not seem to make much difference either. Both Brazil and India had relatively small numbers of foreign students at the study institutions in comparison to some of the other countries, yet respondents in Brazil and India were at the top of the list in terms of reporting that they were predominantly in the company of Brazilian and Indian students (64.1 percent and 63.0 percent respectively). Kenya, where there were relatively few foreign students, was just slightly behind the United States in this respect. There were a large number of foreign students at the American study institutions. At the same time, 65 percent of the respondents in the Federal Republic of Germany reported that when they were in the company of others, the others were mainly German students. The location of the universities, in an urban or in a more rural and isolated setting, did not seem to have influenced this variable.

TABLE 5.1

Friends and Contact with Others, Part I
(in percentages)

	Brazil	Canada	France	Hong Kong	India	Iran	Japan	Kenya	U.K.	U.S.	W. Germany
When you are in the company of others, are they mainly:											
Local (name) students	64.1	24.0	13.0	17.0	63.0	29.0	40.0	36.0	43.0	41.0	65.0
Local non-students	5.4	8.0	12.0	17.0	0.0	8.0	13.0	12.0	5.0	2.0	10.0
Local (name) family	2.2	1.0	8.0	4.0	0.0	2.0	7.0	1.0	0.0	2.0	0.0
Fellow nationals	9.8	40.0	30.0	48.0	27.0	39.0	13.0	48.0	20.0	34.0	20.0
Other foreign students	18.5	27.0	37.0	13.0	10.0	22.0	27.0	3.0	32.0	22.0	5.0
Regular contact brought about through lodging with:											
Local students	59.1	18.1	16.0	46.7	50.0	31.6	0.0	61.8	54.7	55.5	83.3
Local non-students	10.6	25.8	14.0	33.3	0.0	0.0	20.0	20.6	18.0	7.5	0.0
Local families	15.2	5.5	18.0	13.3	23.3	5.3	20.0	0.0	6.7	5.4	16.7
Fellow nationals	15.2	50.5	52.0	6.7	26.7	63.2	60.0	17.6	20.7	31.6	0.0
Roommate:											
Local student	48.5	14.8	9.5	92.9	29.6	7.1	*	88.5	47.8	53.5	40.0
Fellow national	27.3	54.8	52.4	7.1	55.6	64.3		11.5	26.1	25.8	20.0
Other foreigner	24.2	30.4	38.1	0.0	14.8	28.6		0.0	26.1	20.7	40.0

*Comparable data were not available from Japan for this item.

Source: Compiled by the authors.

In other words, while no clear pattern emerged from the data, it does seem evident that certain countries exhibit much less interaction than others between foreign and native students. To illustrate this point, the data presented for the French sample indicated that only 13 percent of the foreign students in France reported that when they were in the company of others, those others were mainly French students. This was the lowest percentage among all of the 11 countries participating in this international investigation.

It could fairly be argued that the item itself might be too vague and complex, even though this did not appear to be the case in the pilot testing. A variable was introduced, however,* to determine what kind of contact—in terms of nationals versus non-nationals—would be evident if the focus was on the reported contact brought about by lodging patterns. It certainly seems logical to argue that student respondents are more likely to have contact with those who live around them and whom they would be expected to encounter during the regular course of the day at the place where they live. This variable included four options rather than the five discussed above. These options were local individuals (local students, non-students, or families) and fellow nationals.

The data again indicated that in certain countries more than half of the respondents reported regular contact with fellow nationals through their place of residence. Specifically, 63.2 percent of the respondents in Iran reported regular contact mainly with fellow nationals, as did 60.0 percent in Japan, 52.0 percent in France, and 50.5 percent in Canada. Respondents studying in France also reported the least contact with local students, 16.0 percent.

There are, of course, complications relating to any variable. For example, resident patterns of foreign students certainly vary according to the available facilities at educational institutions, in terms of reserving advanced space in residences for newly arriving foreign students. International houses, pensions, apartments, and so forth vary country by country. Nevertheless, it is important to notice that in both this analysis and that presented immediately

---

*Respondents were asked to specify "With which of the following groups (does) your present lodging bring you into regular contact": local (name) students, fellow nationals, local (name) non-students, a (name) family, or other. For each option, the respondent was given the option of listing "yes" or "no." The data were then grouped to consider those who indicated "yes" for "local students" but "no" on all other options, etc.

above—dealing with those in whose company the respondents were mainly spending their time—France, Iran, and Canada could be distinguished as samples with less contact between native and foreign students than reported in the other countries. Or, to make the opposite point, these were the countries with more evident contact between foreign student respondents and other foreigners.

The data (Table 5.1) also indicate that the roommate or individual(s) with whom the respondent was sharing the particular lodging was least likely to be a local student in the following countries: 7.1 percent in Iran were with a local student, 9.5 percent in France, and 14.8 percent in Canada. Again, France, Canada, and Iran could be distinguished, this time easily, in this respect from the other participating countries.

Conversely, 92.9 percent of the respondents in Iran, 90.5 percent in France, and 85.2 percent in Canada were sharing lodging, in some form, with either fellow nationals or with other foreign students. Once again, France, Canada, and Iran emerged with this pattern.

It should also be noted that there were other countries where more than 50 percent of the respondents were sharing lodgings with either fellow nationals or other foreign students: India had 70.4 percent, the Federal Republic of Germany 60.0 percent, the United Kingdom 52.2 percent, and Brazil 51.5 percent (data were unavailable for Japan). Again it should be recalled that residence patterns are influenced by affordable options known or available to foreign students at sojourn locations. All that can be fairly noted as out of line here is, to repeat, that France, Canada, and Iran distinguished themselves in the present data by their higher levels of contact between foreign students and other non-natives, and by their lower levels of contact between foreign students and natives.

We are not necessarily implying that there always "ought to be" more contact between native people and foreign students. Not everyone wants social contact with others, let alone with native individuals. Certainly students have the right to choose to be completely alone if that is, in fact, what they wish. We, therefore, also asked the respondents whether their contacts with the native people were "as frequent" or "less frequent" than they wished.

As shown in Table 5.2, respondents in general judged their contacts with native people to be as frequent as they wished in Kenya, the Federal Republic of Germany, Brazil, the United Kingdom, India, Japan, and the United States. More than half of the respondents so indicated in the samples for those particular countries. Those who were least likely to report that their contact was as frequent as they wished were in France (28.0 percent), Hong Kong (39.0 percent), Canada (46.5 percent), and Iran (48.6 percent). The

TABLE 5.2

Friends and Contact with Others, Part II
(in percentages)

	Brazil	Canada	France	Hong Kong	India	Iran	Japan	Kenya	U.K.	U.S.	W. Germany
Since your arrival, have you made any good friends?											
Yes	87.8	87.2	68.1	90.5	89.1	75.3	90.0	97.6	88.3	88.8	81.6
No	12.2	12.8	31.9	9.5	10.9	24.7	10.0	2.4	11.7	11.2	18.4
Nationality of your "best friend" in this country:											
Local student	51.0	21.0	15.0	21.0	33.0	31.0	35.0	28.0	37.0	35.0	41.4
Local non-student	4.0	12.0	13.0	14.0	4.0	4.0	25.0	17.0	5.0	5.0	13.8
Local family	5.0	2.0	3.0	0.0	9.0	8.0	5.0	1.0	3.0	5.0	6.9
Fellow national	18.0	38.0	42.0	57.0	46.0	41.0	15.0	53.0	29.0	35.0	17.2
Other foreigner	21.0	27.0	28.0	7.0	9.0	12.0	20.0	1.0	27.0	20.0	20.7
Are your contacts with (name) people:											
As frequent as you wish?	68.5	46.5	28.0	39.0	60.7	48.6	60.0	78.6	61.0	51.6	74.0
Less frequent than you wish?	31.5	53.5	72.0	61.0	39.3	52.4	40.0	21.4	39.0	48.4	26.0

Source: Compiled by the authors.

reverse was, of course, true with regard to those indicating that their contacts with native people were less frequent than they wished. Again, France, Canada, and Iran could be distinguished together, but this time Hong Kong was added.

Further analysis is needed of the relations between the foreign student respondents in each of these participating countries and native individuals. It could be argued that what would be most important for an individual coping within a foreign culture is not just contact with native individuals but whether or not they have made good friends—a factor presumably more closely associated with the modified culture contact hypothesis. In fact, much of the past research on foreign student adjustment has looked at whether or not the foreign student had "good friends."

The assumption is that foreign students with at least one "good friend" are likely to have an easier time coping with and adjusting to the sojourn culture and to the foreign educational institutions because they still have someone with whom to share joys as well as sorrows and with whom difficulties can be worked through. It can be argued that students who really do consider themselves alone, even if by deliberate choice, do not have the same support available for living within the sojourn culture of the host institution. For example, as one student put it:

> I came to this country to secure my Ph.D. degree
> and have done nothing but study and attend to my
> work since arriving here. I am not interested in
> meeting anyone until I finish what I came here for.
> I am pleased with myself and my progress so far.

That student, seemingly coping well with the tasks that have brought him to the foreign institution, is alone by choice.

Our respondents were asked if they had made any "good friends" specifically "since your arrival" (see Table 5.2). Everywhere the majority answer was clearly "yes." However, those least likely to say "yes," or conversely, those most likely to say "no," were in France and Iran. In France, 31.9 percent of the respondents indicated that they had not made any "good friends" and in Iran the figure was 24.7 percent. This item did not distinguish between native and foreign friends. It referred to having made "any good friends" in general.

Admittedly, a "good friend" is another rather general category, and hence the focus of this international investigation moved to the "best friend." Asking the foreign student respondent to specify the "best friend in this country" required, again, a forced-choice response. Furthermore, our interest here centers not on the name or the qualities that make the selected individual the "best friend," but rather the native versus foreigner distinction. Is the "best friend" a local individual (student, non-student, or family), a fellow national, or another foreigner?

As might be expected, some respondents indicated that they did not have a "best friend" in the sojourn country and left the item blank. Others indicated that they had several "very good friends" but no one friend that would stand out from the others. Still others indicated that they just could not limit their response to a single individual. Again, the analyses were completed only for those respondents who did respond to the forced-choice item and specified the nationality of their "best friend" in the sojourn country.

In eight of the country samples, more than half of the respondents indicated that their "best friend" was either a fellow national or another foreigner. This was so for 70 percent in France, 65 percent in Canada, 64 percent in Hong Kong, 56 percent in the United Kingdom, 55 percent in both India and the United States, 54 percent in Kenya, and 53 percent in Iran. In this analysis, France and Iran led the list with the most fellow national or other foreign "best friends."

Respondents naming a local student as their "best friend" were the most likely to be in Brazil (51 percent) or the Federal Republic of Germany (41.4 percent). It is worth noting that only in the case of Brazil did more than half of the responding sample indicate that their "best friend" was a local student.

France had the lowest percentage indicating that their "best friend" was a local student (15 percent), followed by Canada and Hong Kong (both with 21.0 percent). Thus, with regard to this particular item, France and Canada are distinguished by the relative absence of relationships between the foreign respondents and local students. Iran is more within the range that was reported generally, but Hong Kong emerged as similar to Canada, as it had in one previous relationship discussed above. Hence, the picture that continues to emerge is one of an absence of contact between the foreign students and native people; it emerges regularly in France and slightly less regularly but is clearly evident in Canada, Iran, and Hong Kong.

The specific patterns that emerged in these data with regard to France, Canada, Iran, and Hong Kong and that have been repeated throughout this discussion, should not, however, obscure the overall point that contact between foreign students and local individuals varies widely from country to country, but the evidence does suggest that there is a relatively large number of foreign students who would welcome more contact than they were at that point reporting.

BEHAVIORAL INDICATORS IN SOCIAL CONTACT

The question of personal interaction between foreign students and those native to the sojourn country, either inside or outside the host institution, needs to be approached not only with regard to various aspects of social contact and friendship, as discussed in the preceding section, but also in terms of what kind of behavioral contact has occurred and how frequently. While the specific behaviors that can be studied are limitless, for the purposes of this present investigation only social and indirect behavioral factors that should bring foreign students together with native people were selected. The progression of items was as follows: opportunities for social contact with local families; invitations to visit them; walks, outings, or evenings with families; doing academic work in cooperation with local individuals; involvement in community activities; artistic and social activities; the opportunity to discuss what the respondent considered to be "significant issues" with native individuals; "positive contact" with neighbors; and meals with neighbors. All of these activities require some specific behavioral interaction between the foreign students and individuals native to the sojourn country. Additional indirect aspects of culture contact between foreign students and the sojourn culture were also considered. For example, reading national newspapers and magazines; watching local television; and going to museums or exhibitions—all of these are ways in which the host culture can make an impact on foreign students (and vice versa presumedly if there are enough foreign students in the host community).

Again, within an international investigation, local conditions and options will influence the situation; in addition, the selection of educational institutions in each of the participating countries had to be made so that we could count on the options being available to the foreign students. However, it is impossible to follow students around to make sure that the behaviors were truthfully reported, and it was obvious that in some countries certain options are more widely available than in others. For example, television is common in the United States and at all of the U.S. study institutions, with numerous channels offering programs around the clock, but in Hong Kong, television is limited, with programs in Chinese and English and with a large number of American reruns. In London, there are three channels, and they broadcast only within specific periods of the day.

The mean responses to the questions asked in this context require careful study (see Table 5.3). The means were calculated on a scale of "very often" with a numerical value of 1 through "never" with a numerical value of 5. Omit responses were not used in calculating the means.

What was noted in the preceding section is again evident here. In almost every case relating to contact between foreign student respondents and natives, France and Canada regularly rank among the countries with the least frequent or regular contact. Iran usually ranks lower than most of the other countries. Hong Kong ranks lowest in terms of local newspapers and magazines read, local television programs watched, and also low in terms of museums or exhibitions visited.

Possibly more important, however, is the relatively small amount of contact between foreign students and native individuals in respect to these items. For example, opportunities for social contact with families are at best reported to occur "sometimes" with only those in Brazil reporting opportunities as being relatively frequent. Invitations to visit local families again come "sometimes." The opportunity to discuss what the respondents consider to be significant issues with native individuals can also be best described as "sometimes," although this seems to occur more frequently in Kenya and the Federal Republic of Germany. Positive contact with neighbors also seems to occur "sometimes," although more frequently in Kenya, and the Federal Republic of Germany. Meals shared with natives in the neighborhood are again "sometimes."

"Sometimes" in terms of an average response to this type of item could be evaluated as indicating that things were fine. This evaluation is unwarranted, however, in the light of the large number of comments written into the margins and at the end of the instrument that suggest again and again that more contact and interaction with native people would be desirable.

Again and again, when asked for suggestions to improve the sojourn experience, students ask for help in meeting and interacting with local individuals. "Just to have a reception line at the beginning of the year to shake hands with the President is not enough," said one respondent. "I need someone to help me get involved with other students or in clubs with [local] students; I know that I should be able to do this sort of thing myself, but I need help," said another. "The host family seems to have worked for a friend of mine, but all my host family did was invite me for dinner once and drove me around the city. I wanted to be able to talk to them and to feel free to drop in but we did not seem to have anything in common."

In fact, the above items (minus those concerning newspapers, television programs, and museums) seemed to act in concert. That is, if students had more contact with local individuals on one of the items, they tended to report more contact on all the items. The reverse was also true: those with less contact (reporting "never") tended to be those with less contact throughout.

Interestingly enough, those students most likely to be dissatisfied overall with regard to other than academic aspects of their

TABLE 5.3

Social and Indirect Contact with Those Native to the Sojourn Country

	Brazil	Canada	France	Hong Kong	India	Iran	Japan	Kenya	U.K.	U.S.	W. Germany
Do you have opportunities for social contact with (name of country) families?	2.231	3.373	3.545	3.475	3.357	3.222	2.828	3.048	3.098	2.997	2.707
Have you ever been invited to visit ( )* families?	2.322	3.476	3.547	3.512	3.473	3.282	3.103	2.905	3.136	3.003	2.585
Do you go for walks, outings, or evenings with ( )?	2.728	3.183	3.385	3.025	3.321	3.507	3.138	2.012	2.594	3.117	2.000
Do you do academic work in cooperation with ( )?	2.546	2.900	3.716	3.610	2.929	3.208	2.893	1.345	2.913	2.961	3.512
Are you involved in community activities with ( )?	3.493	4.007	4.179	4.195	3.927	3.859	3.536	4.289	3.888	4.050	3.146
Are you collaborating on an artistic function or social activity with ( )?—theatrical performance, film club, or social action.	3.897	4.064	4.043	4.000	3.891	4.186	4.071	4.289	3.942	4.290	3.000

64

Question											
Do you have the opportunity to discuss what you consider to be significant issues with ( )?	2.674	2.985	3.096	3.000	3.273	3.597	3.069	1.393	2.605	2.968	2.049
Do you have positive contacts with neighbors at your apartment, hotel, pension, and so on?	2.623	3.043	3.200	3.049	2.500	3.229	3.667	1.759	2.551	2.949	2.146
Do you have meals with ( ) in your neighborhood?	2.918	3.631	3.713	3.463	3.264	3.833	4.034	2.369	3.140	3.361	2.707
Do you read ( ) newspapers and magazines?	1.709	2.044	1.768	4.000	1.661	2.366	1.767	1.389	1.842	1.832	2.024
Do you watch ( ) television programs?	2.385	2.413	2.716	3.800	3.582	2.740	1.633	3.393	2.311	2.106	2.634
Do you go to ( ) museums or exhibitions?	2.878	3.026	2.495	3.051	2.946	2.847	2.933	3.369	2.422	2.791	2.634

Note: The above figures represent the means responses for each country sample on a scale of "very often" (value of 5) through "never" (value of 1). Omit responses were not used in the calculation of the means.

*"( )" indicates "fill in name of country."

Source: Compiled by the authors.

65

sojourn (Table 3.5 in Chapter 3), in terms of mean responses, were the most likely to have been studying in Iran, followed by France, then India, and then Canada. It was also true that, again in terms of mean responses, those students most likely to be dissatisfied overall with regard to their studies were the most likely to have been studying in Hong Kong, followed by Japan, then France, then Iran, the Federal Republic of Germany, or Canada.

Does contact play a significant part in a respondent's coping and adapting processes as well as in an overall self-assessment as proposed in the modified culture contact hypothesis? Certainly the hypothesis deserves further study and will be addressed as the discussion now progresses to other aspects of coping and adapting in a foreign university.

NOTES

1. C. Selltiz et al., Attitudes and Social Relations of Foreign Students in the United States (Minneapolis: University of Minnesota Press, 1963).

2. Hwa-Bao Chang, "Attitudes of Chinese Students in the United States," Sociology and Social Research 58 (1973): 66-77.

3. Saad E. M. Ibrahim, "Interaction, Perception, and Attitudes of Arab Students Toward American," Sociology and Social Research 55 (1970): 29-46.

4. A. K. Basu and Richard G. Ames, "Cross-Cultural Contact and Attitude Formation," Sociology and Social Research 55 (1970): 5-16.

6

THE "STRANGER":
NATIONAL AND
ETHNIC RELATIONS

The hypothesis that was raised in the preceding chapter with regard to the social contact of foreign students with native or local individuals requires much more discussion: Is such contact a self-generating variable that can influence, in a snowball-like way, the total sojourn and the student's perception of it? Others have recognized this potential, as was noted, with regard to attitudes and attitude change, but the coping and adaptation process must be considered more widely. An important writer who should not be overlooked here is Robert B. Zajonc, who has dealt with the foreign student in terms of "the stranger."

Writing in 1952, Zajonc defined the "stranger" as "a visitor to a country which becomes his temporary domicile, but which was not the locus of his socialization."[1] Zajonc saw the process, which in our discussion has been referred to as coping, as one that will naturally force the "stranger" into being at odds with the host culture, for:

(a) the stranger is to some extent expected to conform to the norms of the host culture; (b) because the stranger's superego stems from another culture, conformity to a new pattern may prove disturbing; (c) because the stranger occupies a uniquely endowed role in the host society, he can enjoy a certain exemption from conformity, and even a certain freedom of aggression against norms.[2]

He then went on to hypothesize that "given the need to conform, attitudinal aggression of the stranger is a function of his difficulty in conformity," "that attitudinal aggression as a result of frustration in conformity will be greater for strangers with long residence than for those with short residence," and that "strangers with long residence should exhibit lesser need to conform than those with short residence."[3]

Following some preliminary investigations with respect to 30 male foreign students from various countries, Zajonc studied 40 male Indian students, 20 of whom had been in the United States between 6 to 24 months on student visas and expected to return to India, the other 20 being male Indian students with less than six months' stay in the United States but who were also on student visas and expected to return to India.

Zajonc's conclusion is interesting in terms of the coping process:

> . . . the relationship between attitudinal aggression and difficulty in conformity is subject to a developmental process. The sequence of this process is probably the following: need to conform is frustrated by difficulty in conformity; this frustration results in aggression facilitated by the social position of the stranger; aggression against behavioral patterns diminishes the original need to conform in acting as a mechanism of rationalization.[4]

The point appears to be well taken. Certainly, the feelings of the foreign student with regard to conformity to the host culture and frustrations at being unable to do so smoothly and easily might lead to expressions of aggression against the host culture ("aggressive attitudes," in Zajonc's terms), and it is to be expected that these issues will resolve themselves with time. Yet the question of social contact with local individuals may play an important role with regard to entry, or "conformity" in Zajonc's terms, to being comfortable and satisfied with the host culture. Is frustration due to conformity lessened through positive and satisfying social contact with native individuals? The question should be kept open at this point.

There are others who have studied this problem and have reached a widely known hypothesis, which requires consideration in our discussion as well.

THE NATIONAL STATUS HYPOTHESIS

Various writers, among them Richard T. Morris,[5] have noted that the way in which a foreign student views his home country in relation to his host country (the United States) will influence that student's attitudes and adjustment in the host country. The student who views his home country as being lower in status compared with his host country will have a completely different attitude from those who attribute higher status to their own country and undergo, therefore, a completely different adjustment pattern or coping process. To extrapolate further, this could be expected to influence the conformity desires that Zajonc considered important, but in this case the student's perception of the "national status" of his country of origin would be considered more important than the desire for conformity to the host culture or social contact with those native to the sojourn culture. However, the national status hypothesis has not been tested adequately internationally and for good reason.

Ideally, to investigate the "national status hypothesis" one should have studied the foreign student respondents prior to their arrival in the sojourn country and should have determined in advance their attitudes toward the host country in relation to their home country.

In the present 11-nation investigation with limited resources, that was simply impossible, even though it was considered at length. Another approach to the hypothesis would argue that one can place various countries in terms of "high" or "low" on an international ranking in terms of some sort of prestige status. The problem with this approach is that it requires someone to establish rankings of countries without clear guidance as to what factors should be used in determining the rankings. Is one to depend on gross national product, national standards of living, mortality rates, or something less amenable to hard statistics? More importantly, such a ranking, even if available, would still be largely irrelevant, for the issue is not an objective ranking of nations but rather the perceptions of particular foreign students of their own nations in comparison to their host nations, a highly individual judgment.

For the purposes of this present investigation, an attempt was made to secure a measure of respondents' opinions in two specific areas: (1) Had they found that the local population had a reasonably accurate knowledge of their home country, and (2) what, in general, was their attitude toward their (the foreign students') home country?

The responses to these two items are reported in Table 6.1. In general, the respondents did not feel that local individuals had a "reasonably accurate knowledge" of their home country. "No," said 88.3 percent of the students in Brazil, 87.8 percent in the United States, 83.5 percent in France, 77.2 percent in Canada, and so forth. In no country did more than half of the responding sample say "yes."

Cross tabulations of the data on this item produced a clearer understanding of the respondents who felt that the local people had

TABLE 6.1

Perceived Attitude of the Native People toward the Respondents' Country
(in percentages)

	Brazil	Canada	France	Hong Kong	India	Iran	Japan	Kenya	U.K.	U.S.	West Germany
In your experience here, have you found that (name) people have a reasonably accurate knowledge of your country?											
Yes	11.7	22.8	16.5	33.3	21.4	24.7	20.0	47.5	32.2	12.2	47.5
No	88.3	77.2	83.5	66.7	78.6	75.3	80.0	52.5	67.5	87.8	52.5
In general, is the attitude of the (name) people toward your country:											
Very favorable	9.6	4.4	7.6	17.5	17.9	12.3	0.0	13.0	9.1	7.0	17.1
Favorable	37.7	28.0	34.8	40.0	46.4	43.8	20.7	16.0	32.6	25.0	41.5
Neutral	42.5	46.6	35.9	37.5	28.6	27.4	48.3	16.0	41.7	50.0	24.4
Unfavorable	7.5	17.8	17.4	5.0	5.4	12.3	24.1	39.0	15.1	15.0	14.6
Very unfavorable	2.7	3.2	4.3	0.0	1.8	4.1	6.9	16.0	1.4	4.0	2.4

Source: Compiled by the authors.

a reasonably accurate knowledge of their own home countries.* It was found that they were most likely to have origins in the United States and least likely to be from Latin America, the Far East, black African, or Arabic-speaking countries. This might be considered evidence in favor of the "national status hypothesis." They were also most likely to be in the "medium" or "low" contact groups. Thus it could also be argued that these respondents really had little opportunity to find out what knowledge the local people had of their home countries. It should be added that those in the "high" contact group were more likely to feel that the local people did not have a reasonably accurate knowledge of their home countries. This may mean that it is only after considerable contact that a student is able to make fair assessments in this area.

Those who felt that the local people had a reasonably accurate knowledge of their home countries were also likely to indicate that when they were in the company of others, the others were local students, and to report that their "best friend" in the host country was a local student. Their place of residence was likely to be shared with a local student. They were "sometimes" or "rarely" lonely or homesick, neither high nor low in terms of problems reported, had seldom reported a personal experience of being discriminated against in the host country, had rarely indicated that personal depression was a problem, and were more likely to be satisfied with the nonacademic aspects of their sojourns. They were also more likely to rate the teaching quality at the sojourn institution as "satisfactory." It could thus be pointed out that it was social contact with local students, in contrast to social contact with local people, that seems to be reflected in their conclusions regarding the accuracy of the local people's knowledge of their home country.

The patterns of response with regard to the general attitude of native people toward the respondents' home countries varied but showed no clear common tendencies. Those countries that were characterized by the absence of social contact between the foreign student and local individuals—France, Canada, Iran, and Hong Kong—did not clearly differ from others.

Cross tabulations indicated that those who felt the attitude of the local people toward their home country was more favorable were also most likely to have origins in Canada, Australia, New Zealand, the United Kingdom, and Western Europe and least likely to come from black Africa, South East Asia, Arabic-speaking countries,

---

*Data are presented in Chapter Appendix A. Please refer to Chapter 11 for details of the cross tabulation analyses and variables used.

Iran, and South Asia.* They were more likely to be in the group with "more contact" with local people, to be sharing their place of residence with either a local student or their spouse, to indicate that when they were in the company of others, those others were local students or non-students, and to report that a local student was their "best friend" in the sojourn country. They were also more likely to report few difficulties, little loneliness or homesickness, and no experience of personal discrimination, were less likely to check personal depression as a problem, and rated more satisfactorily both the academic and nonacademic aspects of their sojourns overall.

It is possible to argue that this evidence favors a national status hypothesis as being the operating factor. It seems equally likely, however, that the important factor might be the contact with local people. Certainly, there is more evidence in our data for the latter notion than for the national status hypothesis, but the question is by no means answered.

It is possible to approach the whole area from the perspective of the opinion that the foreign students said they had of local people prior to their arrival as well as at the point of the research (mid-academic year). As the data indicate (see Table 6.2), there was a slight trend in most of the samples from a "favorable" to a more "neutral" opinion. This was true of all country samples with the exception of Japan and Kenya, where the opinion of the local people became slightly more positive. In Brazil it remained relatively stable and favorable between both points. In the cases of these countries, however, the differences were very slight.

It should be pointed out that those foreign student respondents with the least favorable opinion of the local people—although the "least favorable opinion" was, in fact, a "neutral" rather than a negative opinion—were found in France, followed by Japan, Canada, and so forth.

Cross tabulations with both items indicated agreement in the data.† The opinion of local people prior to arrival or at the point of research did not, however, correlate with a high, medium, or low personal impact as a result of living in the host country. The respondents' prior opinion also did not correlate with those with whom lodging was shared, with those reporting or not reporting personal depression, or with the reported degrees of loneliness or homesickness. These results require further investigation.

---

*Data are presented in Chapter Appendix B.
†Data are presented in Chapter Appendixes C and D.

TABLE 6.2

Opinion of the Native People

	Brazil	Canada	France	Hong Kong	India	Iran	Japan	Kenya	U.K.	U.S.	West Germany
What was your opinion of the (name) people before you arrived here?	1.913	2.220	2.168	2.167	2.250	2.082	2.700	1.857	2.082	2.275	2.244
What is your opinion of the (name) people today?	1.946	2.464	2.734	2.381	2.375	2.278	2.667	1.843	2.203	2.333	2.333

Note: The above figures represent the means responses for each country sample on a scale of "very favorable" (value of 1) through "very unfavorable" (value of 5). Omit responses were not used in the calculation of the means.

Source: Compiled by the authors.

Those reporting holding a more favorable opinion of local people prior to arrival were most likely to have origins in Eastern Europe, then the United States, Canada, and the South Pacific countries. They were satisfied with the helpfulness of the teachers and the quality of the instruction. They were less likely to report personal discrimination and indicated few difficulties or problems. They were more likely to have traveled prior to arrival in the sojourn country. They were also the most likely to name a local student or non-student as their "best friend" in the sojourn country and to say that when they were in the company of others, the others were more likely to be local students. Overall, they were very satisfied both academically and nonacademically with their experiences at the foreign university.

Those reporting a more favorable opinion of local people at the point of the research were most likely to have their origins in the South Pacific countries, the United Kingdom, Canada, and the United States. In general, they expressed opinions similar to those reported above, but their lodging was more likely to be shared with a local student or non-student, they were less likely to report loneliness or homesickness and to indicate that personal depression was a greater problem or difficulty for them than those with a less favorable opinion of the local people at the point of the research.

Again, one might argue that the above supports, in part, a national status hypothesis, but this is not necessarily the case. Both groups reporting favorable opinions also had more social contact with local people, had local students for their "best friends" in the sojourn country, and indicated that when they were in the company of others, the others were more likely to be local students or non-students. It is thus equally reasonable to argue that what is operating with regard to the attitudes of the foreign students toward the local people is that a higher degree of contact with local people and students has translated into a more favorable opinion—and possibly a better understanding and knowledge—of local people.

All of this, however, is only indirect evidence with regard to the operation of a national status hypothesis internationally. All that can be said is that if the hypothesis does operate internationally, two possibilities must be recognized: (1) the present study, its methodology and instruments, did not prove to be sensitive enough to locate the evidence for or against the hypothesis, or (2) the hypothesis is of such a special nature that it requires a detailed longitudinal investigation beginning in the home culture, which we were unable to accomplish even though such was originally considered.

The case study analyses did not indicate, it should be added, a great deal that would substantiate the national status hypothesis. On the other hand, they do support our earlier argument: Significant

culture contact with local individuals is, in reality, more crucial
to coping and adaptation than the perceived national status of the
student's home nation with regard to the host nation.

LONELINESS AND HOMESICKNESS

Another way of looking at conformity patterns, in Zajonc's
terms, is to consider expressions of loneliness and homesickness in
the respondents. While this was included in the present investigation, the results do not add appreciably to what was already known.
Some students are certainly lonely and homesick. Those less lonely
and homesick tend to have their spouses present with them in the
sojourn country. However, we have no statistically significant evidence of a direct correlation between the presence of a spouse and
the absence of loneliness or homesickness.

In the present investigation, respondents were the least likely
to be lonely in Japan, and the most likely to be so in France. However, they were the most likely to report homesickness in either
Iran or Brazil and the least likely in Japan. In general, "sometimes" and "rarely" were by far the most common responses with
regard to loneliness and homesickness. However, in terms of percentage responses, it is worth noting that 21.4 percent of the sample
in India reported being lonely "very often," as did 16 percent in
France. Similarly, 16.1 percent in India reported being homesick
"very often," as did 13.7 percent in Iran, 10.8 percent in Brazil,
9.5 percent in France, and 7.6 percent in Canada.

The patterns that were visible, however, overwhelmingly
showed distributions that peaked in the "sometimes" and "rarely"
areas for both items. This would seem to indicate that the variables
did not discriminate enough to make further analyses and interpretation fruitful with the present samples and may also indicate that future research will probably not find this variable among the most
pertinent to international foreign student adjustment. The two items
were significantly correlated between themselves, as they mean almost the same thing.

DISCRIMINATION

In dealing with conformity pressures and accepting Zajonc's
notion that the "stranger" can be expected to react aggressively to
those things within the host culture which tend to offend, the attempt
was made to ascertain whether prejudice or discrimination was being felt by the foreign students in particular countries. The word

TABLE 6.3

Loneliness and Homesickness

	Brazil	Canada	France	Hong Kong	India	Iran	Japan	Kenya	U.K.	U.S.	West Germany
Loneliness:											
1. Very often	6.1%	6.5%	16.0%	4.9%	21.4%	11.0%	3.4%	7.1%	3.3%	7.2%	2.4%
2. Often	10.9%	10.8%	11.7%	7.3%	3.6%	13.7%	0.0%	8.3%	6.0%	9.2%	7.1%
3. Sometimes	48.3%	45.0%	44.7%	53.7%	32.1%	46.6%	44.8%	34.5%	39.1%	43.3%	38.1%
4. Rarely	21.1%	24.8%	22.3%	22.0%	26.8%	17.8%	20.7%	44.0%	29.1%	23.8%	35.7%
5. Never	13.6%	12.9%	5.3%	12.2%	16.1%	11.0%	31.0%	6.0%	22.6%	16.5%	16.7%
Mean	3.3	3.3	2.9	3.3	3.1	3.0	3.8	3.3	3.6	3.3	3.6
Homesickness:											
1. Very often	10.8%	7.6%	9.5%	0.0%	16.1%	13.7%	0.0%	4.8%	1.6%	5.6%	0.0%
2. Often	23.0%	8.4%	11.6%	11.9%	10.7%	19.2%	3.6%	8.3%	4.3%	7.6%	9.8%
3. Sometimes	44.6%	41.4%	45.3%	33.3%	37.5%	50.7%	35.7%	40.5%	29.6%	45.7%	34.1%
4. Rarely	18.2%	30.4%	13.7%	38.1%	17.9%	11.0%	32.1%	40.5%	40.8%	28.9%	46.3%
5. Never	3.2%	12.1%	20.0%	16.7%	17.9%	5.5%	28.6%	6.0%	23.6%	12.2%	9.8%
Mean	2.8	3.3	3.2	3.6	3.1	2.8	3.9	3.3	3.8	3.3	3.6

Source: Compiled by the authors.

"prejudice," however, was judged during the pilot testing as being too broad, emotionally loaded, and complex. It was consequently avoided. Instead, students were asked about "discrimination."

Students were questioned concerning five distinctly separate areas with regard to discrimination:

1. Before your first visit to this country, did you think that foreign students IN GENERAL would be discriminated against or disliked here because of their nationality, religion, or color?

_____ yes

_____ no

_____ I had no opinion before my first visit to this country

2. Before your first visit to this country, did you think that students from YOUR OWN country would be discriminated against or disliked in this country because of their nationality, religion, or color?

_____ yes

_____ no

_____ I had no opinion before my first visit to this country

3. Since your arrival in this country, have you found more or less discrimination than you expected?

_____ more than what I expected

_____ less than what I expected

_____ about what I expected

_____ I had no expectations in this area

4. Do you have friends or relatives who have experienced discrimination in this country?

_____ yes

_____ no

5. Have you personally had the experience of being discriminated against in this country?

_____ yes

_____ no

The point of this range of items on discrimination was to attempt to distinguish the presence of perceived discrimination as well as the respondents' expectations, pre-arrival attitudes, and personal experiences.

The initial two items elicited few data that proved illuminating. Most respondents either reported "no opinion" or had not felt that foreign students in general would be discriminated against in the sojourn country. Those reporting "yes" were most likely in France

(31.3 percent), the United States (22.4 percent), the United Kingdom (19.6 percent), and Canada (19.1 percent)—minority opinions, certainly. The same was true with regard to the expectation that foreign students from the respondents' own countries would be discriminated against in the sojourn country. Those reporting "yes" were again most likely in France (19.8 percent), then Hong Kong (19.0 percent), Canada (18.7 percent), the United States (18.0 percent), and Kenya (17.9 percent)—again, minority opinions. More than half of each country sample reported that they had not expected to find discrimination against students from their home countries. In summary, while some respondents did anticipate discrimination on the basis of nationality, religion, or color, these were clearly in the minority.

In the other areas, more thought-provoking data were found (see Table 6.4). For example, the only country that distinguished itself by having a large percentage of its sample reporting that they had found more discrimination than they had expected since their arrival was France. There 41.5 percent of the foreign students reported that this was their experience. In most country samples, the predominant opinion reported by the respondents was that they had no expectations in the area. This held true for Brazil, Hong Kong, India, Iran, Japan, Kenya, and the Federal Republic of Germany. In the United Kingdom, the United States, and Canada opinion was more evenly divided between having no such expectations and finding about what was expected in terms of discrimination in the sojourn country.

It has been noted elsewhere by Otto Klineberg and J. Ben Brika[6] that Third World students reported more discrimination against friends and relatives in Europe than they had actually experienced themselves. These same phenomena were found to be true of foreign students in Canada, France, Iran, Japan, the United Kingdom, the United States, and the Federal Republic of Germany. Brazil and India ranked equally in regard to discrimination against friends and relatives as well as the personal experience of discrimination. Only in Hong Kong and in Kenya did more respondents report a higher percentage of personal discrimination than that accorded friends or relatives.

The respondents were the most likely to indicate that they had friends or relatives who had experienced discrimination if they were in Japan (53.6 percent said "yes") and were least likely to so indicate in Iran (74.0 percent said "no") or in the Federal Republic of Germany (73.2 percent said "no").

With regard to personal discrimination, in no country did a majority of the respondents report having experienced discrimination personally. The highest percentage was in Japan where 44.4

TABLE 6.4

Perceived Discrimination
(in percentages)

	Brazil	Canada	France	Hong Kong	India	Iran	Japan	Kenya	U.K.	U.S.	West Germany
Since your arrival in this country, have you found more or less discrimination than you expected?											
More	10.9	22.5	41.5	11.9	14.3	21.0	20.7	23.8	24.4	20.2	15.0
Less	12.2	14.5	9.6	14.3	7.1	22.0	24.1	19.0	11.1	15.3	10.0
About what I expected	20.4	31.0	27.7	31.0	12.5	7.0	20.7	19.0	33.5	30.1	23.0
I had no expectations in this area	56.5	32.1	21.3	42.9	66.1	50.0	34.5	38.1	31.0	34.4	51.0
Do you have friends or relatives who have experienced discrimination in this country?											
Yes	11.0	45.9	45.3	28.6	30.4	26.0	53.6	31.0	39.3	41.6	26.8
No	90.0	54.1	54.7	71.4	69.6	74.0	46.4	69.0	60.7	58.4	73.2
Have you personally had the experience of being discriminated against in this country?											
Yes	11.6	34.2	35.8	36.6	30.4	22.2	44.4	34.5	22.0	30.6	17.9
No	88.4	65.7	64.2	63.4	69.6	77.8	55.6	65.5	78.0	69.4	82.1

Source: Compiled by the author.

percent of the respondents so reported. The lowest percentage was in Brazil (11.6 percent).

Thus while it certainly seems to be true that although more foreign students are aware of others who have been discriminated against than have personally felt discrimination themselves, here are foreign students who definitely feel that they are discriminated against in the sojourn country. Furthermore, to the degree that the present country samples are representative, those students who feel discrimination are most likely to be (in descending order) studying in Japan, Hong Kong, France, Kenya, and Canada.

THE "BRAIN DRAIN" AND PREFERENCE TO REMAIN

There has been a great deal of discussion about the migration of trained foreign personnel from one country to another. This is often referred to as the "brain drain" or an "international interchange or migration of talent," depending on one's point of view. It is beyond the scope of this present investigation to study these phenomena, and the technical arguments in this area have been left to others.[7] Nevertheless, it is important to recognize that the students' preference in terms of remaining in the sojourn country is an important indicator as to how the sojourn experience is going. In other words, an unobtrusive measure of Zajonc's point with regard to conformity frustrations leading to aggressive attitudes might be in terms of the foreign student's preference as to whether to remain in or leave the sojourn country.

In this investigation, it is important to realize that the respondents were specifically questioned in the context of "as a result of your experience in this country and if you had the choice. . . ." Pilot testing of the item indicated that foreign student respondents generally felt that they for various reasons did not have a real choice between remaining in the sojourn country or going elsewhere, but they also indicated that they could respond to this item on the assumption that a choice was possible.

Furthermore, they also indicated that they understood that the item was being asked in terms of their "experience" in the sojourn country. There is no way, of course, to be certain that the opinions expressed in the pilot studies were also shared by the foreign students in the various country samples. However, accepted research procedures would certainly allow us to proceed on that assumption.

The respondents were asked to indicate if they would prefer to "stay in this country," "return to your own country," "go to another country," or "no preference." As can be seen from the data (see Table 6.5), the largest percentage in any single category in every

TABLE 6.5

Choice of Residence
(in percentages)

As a result of your experience in this country and if you had the choice, would you prefer to:

	Brazil	Canada	France	Hong Kong	India	Iran	Japan	Kenya	U.K.	U.S.	West Germany
Stay in this country	16.0	17.6	15.7	25.6	13.2	15.0	13.8	10.7	15.0	14.9	15.4
Return to your own country	50.0	53.1	53.9	41.0	52.8	58.0	48.3	81.0	58.0	58.2	43.6
Go to another country	14.0	12.3	14.6	23.1	20.8	17.0	24.1	6.0	14.0	6.0	7.7
No preference	19.0	17.0	15.7	10.3	13.2	10.0	13.8	2.4	14.0	20.9	33.3

Source: Compiled by the authors.

country selected the option to "return to their own country." This was true for half or more of the respondents in 8 of the 11 countries. Those foreign students least likely to express this preference were in Hong Kong. Those more desirous of returning to their own country were in Kenya, followed by those in the United States, then the United Kingdom, and Iran.

Were the students expressing aggressive attitudes toward the sojourn culture by expressing the desire to leave, as Zajonc's research might lead us to expect? Not necessarily. Is the modified culture contact hypothesis more likely to be correct in suggesting that these students were not experiencing adequate social contact and that this led to the frustration, in terms of conformity, with which Zajonc begins? Again, not necessarily. Have we found evidence that the national status hypothesis is operating in these samples? Probably not. Rather, now that this portion of the evidence has been presented, we suggest that it be kept in mind—with the various possible explanations and hypotheses—while more evidence is presented and until a discussion of the intercorrelations within the data can be explored.

In this chapter we have looked at the question of the foreign student as an individual ethnically and culturally distinguishable from those native to the sojourn culture. We have reported on the student's perceptions of loneliness and homesickness as well as discrimination and opinions concerning local people. Only limited support was found for the "national status hypothesis."

NOTES

1. Robert B. Zajonc, "Aggressive Attitudes of the 'Stranger' as a Function of Conformity Pressures," Human Relations 5, no. 2 (1952): 206, footnote 1.

2. Ibid., p. 207.

3. Ibid., p. 208.

4. Ibid., pp. 215-16.

5. Richard T. Morris, The Two-Way Mirror: National Status in Foreign Students' Adjustment (Minneapolis: University of Minnesota Press, 1960). See also: Richard T. Morris, "National Status and Attitudes of Foreign Students," Journal of Social Issues 12 (1956): 20-25; and C. G. McClintock and J. Davis, "Changes in the Attribute of Nationality in the Self-Perception of the Stranger," Journal of Social Psychology 48 (1958): 183-93.

6. Otto Klineberg and J. Ben Brika, Etudiants du Tier-Monde en Europe (Paris: Mouton, 1972).

7. William A. Glaser, Brain Drain and Study Abroad (New York: Columbia University Bureau of Applied Social Research, 1974).

CHAPTER APPENDIXES

Appendix A: Cross Tabulations: The Variable of Local People's Knowledge of Respondents' Home Country

Item: In your experience here, have you found that (name) people have a reasonably accurate knowledge of your country? Yes or no.

	Chi Square	Degrees of Freedom
"Traveled" vs. "nontraveled" respondents	2.763	2
"Lots of contact" vs. "medium" vs. "little contact"	72.989	4*
Geographic "origin" of respondents	379.225	24*
Nationality of others "when in the company of others"	43.147	6*
Nationality of "best friend" in the host country	42.758	6*
Person with whom lodging is shared	18.635	10
"Many" vs. "some" vs. "few" problems or difficulties	29.191	4*
Reporting vs. not reporting personal depression	20.109	2*
Reporting vs. not reporting personal discrimination	34.165	1*
Reported opinion of the local people	78.042	4*
Loneliness	31.502	8*
Homesickness	65.311	8*
Rating of teaching quality at the host institution	40.734	10*
Rating helpfulness of teachers at the host institution	11.392	10
"High" vs. "medium" vs. "low" impact as a result of the experience of living in the host country	6.809	4
Satisfaction vs. dissatisfaction with general regard to studies	14.526	8
Satisfaction vs. dissatisfaction with general regard to other aspects of the sojourn experience	64.669	8*

*Significant at the .01 level.

N.B. The particulars of the cross tabulations are explained in Chapter 11.

Appendix B: Cross Tabulations: The Variable of Local
People's Attitude toward Respondents' Home Country

Item: In general, is the attitude of the (name) people toward your
country: very favorable, favorable, neutral, unfavorable, very unfavorable?
(Analyzed: very favorable/favorable vs. neutral vs. unfavorable/very
unfavorable)

	Chi Square	Degrees of Freedom
"Traveled" vs. "nontraveled" respondents	9.047	2
"Lots of contact" vs. "medium" vs. "little contact"	104.974	4*
Geographic "origin" of respondents	406.835	24*
Nationality of others "when in the company of others"	84.408	6*
Nationality of "best friend" in the host country	88.146	6*
Person with whom lodging is shared	26.063	10*
"Many" vs. "some" vs. "few" problems or difficulties	44.426	4*
Reporting vs. not reporting personal depression	8.323	2
Reporting vs. not reporting personal discrimination	188.271	2*
Reported opinion of the local people	262.719	4*
Loneliness	55.745	8*
Homesickness	44.326	8*
Rating of teaching quality at the host institution	29.471	10*
Rating helpfulness of teachers at the host institution	67.046	10*
"High" vs. "medium" vs. "low" impact as a result of the experience of living in the host country	8.133	4
Satisfaction vs. dissatisfaction with general regard to studies	28.915	8*
Satisfaction vs. dissatisfaction with general regard to other aspects of the sojourn experience	101.261	8*

*Significant at the .01 level.
N.B. The particulars of the cross tabulations are explained in
Chapter 11.

Appendix C: Cross Tabulations: The Variable of
Respondents' Opinion of Local People Prior to Arrival

Item: What was your opinion of the (name) people before you arrived
here? very favorable, favorable, neutral, unfavorable, very unfavorable
(Analyzed: very favorable/favorable vs. neutral vs. unfavorable/very
unfavorable)

	Chi Square	Degrees of Freedom
"Traveled" vs. "nontraveled" respondents	13.885	2*
"Lots of contact" vs. "medium" vs. "little contact"	57.055	4*
Geographic "origin" of respondents	97.221	24*
Nationality of others "when in the company of others"	27.554	5*
Nationality of "best friend" in the host country	20.037	6*
Person with whom lodging is shared	22.392	10
"Many" vs. "some" vs. "few" problems or difficulties	18.219	4*
Reporting vs. not reporting personal depression	2.280	2
Reporting vs. not reporting personal discrimination	11.486	2*
Reported opinion of the local people	302.142	4*
Loneliness	7.342	8
Homesickness	18.156	8
Rating of teaching quality at the host institution	43.301	10*
Rating helpfulness of teachers at the host institution	36.648	10*
"High vs. "medium" vs. "low" impact as a result of the experience of living in the host country	4.440	4
Satisfaction vs. dissatisfaction with general regard to studies	36.272	8*
Satisfaction vs. dissatisfaction with general regard to other aspects of the sojourn experience	45.705	8*

*Significant at the .01 level.
N.B. The particulars of the cross tabulations are explained in
Chapter 11.

Appendix D: Cross Tabulations: The Variable of
Respondents' Opinion of Local People at the Point
of the Research

Item: What is your opinion of the (name) people today? very favorable, favorable, neutral, unfavorable, very unfavorable (Analyzed: very
favorable/favorable vs. neutral vs. unfavorable/very unfavorable)

	Chi Square	Degrees of Freedom
"Traveled" vs. "nontraveled" respondents	12.949	2*
"Lots of contact" vs. "medium" vs. "little contact"	238.391	4*
Geographic "origin" of respondents	129.947	24*
Nationality of others "when in the company of others"	107.377	6*
Nationality of "best friend" in the host country	157.368	6*
Person with whom lodging is shared	35.362	10*
"Many" vs. "some" vs. "few" problems or difficulties	89.609	4*
Reporting vs. not reporting personal depression	42.163	2*
Reporting vs. not reporting personal discrimination	188.926	2*
Reported opinion of the local people	—	—
Loneliness	136.677	8*
Homesickness	72.009	8*
Rating of teaching quality at the host institution	135.442	10*
Rating helpfulness of teachers at the host institution	166.585	10*
"High" vs. "medium" vs. "low" impact as a result of the experience of living in the host country	4.777	4
Satisfaction vs. dissatisfaction with general regard to studies	153.753	8*
Satisfaction vs. dissatisfaction with general regard to other aspects of the sojourn experience	392.895	8*

*Significant at the .01 level.

N.B. The particulars of the cross tabulations are explained in
Chapter 11.

7

CONSEQUENCES OF
THE SOJOURN:
IN PROGRESS AND
IN RETROSPECT

IMPACT IN PROGRESS

Any analysis of the consequences or impact of a sojourn at a foreign university presupposes a decision as to what kinds of consequences are important in the present context. If we wish to go a step further in an attempt to evaluate the sojourn, to determine whether the results are good or bad, satisfactory or unsatisfactory, we must also agree in advance as to the goals of international exchange programs in order to be able to decide whether or not these goals have been realized.

There have been a number of attempts to define the goals; the difficulty is that the goal will vary with the source of the relevant program, with the persons responsible for its administration, and with the objectives of those individuals who participate in it. Many highly industrialized nations, such as the United States, the Union of Soviet Socialist Republics, France, Japan, and the United Kingdom, spend substantial resources on such exchanges, usually in the hope of winning friends in other countries, but also as part of their general programs of technical assistance or cooperation. This latter goal may also represent one of the major motives in the fellowship grants given by the United Nations or its specialized agencies, with the added hope that contact across national boundaries will also contribute to the development of greater international understanding. For individual participants in such exchanges, however, the goals may be much more personal, and they may often be quite irrelevant to the purposes for which the international programs were originally and primarily organized.

In our earlier study, we suggested[1] that for purposes of convenience the assessment of the consequences of the foreign sojourn might be considered under four major headings; for the individual, the university, the nation, and the international community.

At the individual student level, one might ask: Did he get what he came for? Did he pass his examinations or receive the degree that he wanted? Did he enjoy his sojourn abroad? What difficulties did he encounter, and could they have been avoided? Did he grow, in experience, in personality? Did his foreign study help him when he returned? Did it have a favorable influence on his career?[2]

At the university level, the authorities may feel that the enterprise has been successful if a contribution has been made to the training of students who in turn play a useful role in the development process in a Third World country. They may also feel that foreign students contribute something to the university, that they help to educate the local students by introducing new ideas or points of view. At the more senior level, one might ask whether the year abroad has added to the skills which made them more useful on their return to their own university. This in turn might represent a contribution to the native country, if they bring back with them the kinds of technical and scientific competence not previously available. On the international scene, the obvious question would be whether they return with a greater feeling of friendliness to the people and the country of sojourn, and whether they are now more likely to reject their national stereotypes, to be less ethnocentric in their judgments, more international in their outlook.

There is obviously no sharp line of demarcation between these four approaches, since what happens to the individuals during their year or longer abroad will affect the university which they attend or to which they will return, their contribution to their own nation, and their attitude toward other nations. In a study by Eide to which reference has already been made,[3] the experience of students abroad was analyzed in relation to their possible role as "links between cultures," or, in our terms, with regard to the impact of the sojourn on international attitudes and behavior. She writes that if the foreign students are to convey anything to their hosts, they must presumably believe that their hosts are interested in what they have to offer. One question asked of the foreign students in Eide's study was the following: "On the whole, how much were the people of your former host country interested in your country?" The percentage answering "very much interested" varied from a high of 74 percent given by Egyptian students who had been in the Federal Republic of Germany, to a low of 25 percent for Iranians in the United Kingdom. In general, all three groups found most interest among the West Germans and least in the United Kingdom; Egyptians were most apt to report interest in their country, with the Indians second and the Iranians last.

Without attempting the difficult task of deciding to what extent these judgments were accurate, we are certainly justified in concluding that the role of culture carrier will not arouse much enthusiasm among those—substantial in number—who find little or no interest in their potential audience. There remains the fact that about half of these foreign students do perceive such interest in their hosts. The question then arises: Did the students have the opportunity to inform their hosts about their home country? Those who said they had "many opportunities" to do so varied from 70 percent for Egyptians in the United States down to only 12 percent for Iranians in the United Kingdom. Usually, but not consistently, high interest goes with many opportunities (correlation coefficient of 0.65). As to the media used, it is clear that for all groups wherever they have been, "informal communication ranks first or second among reported efforts at 'culture carrying' . . . a high proportion mention the informal conversations to be one of the main forms."[4]

The most important "cultural link" refers to the reverse form of communication, that is to say, the impact of the host culture on the foreign student. To a certain extent, this variety of impact is inevitable. The surrounding culture must affect students who live in the host country, and who must make some adjustment to it if they are to succeed. This appears to be true not only for adjustment to the university, since more than 50 percent in all three visiting groups felt that they had become better informed regarding the mentality, customs, and life of the people in the host countries. This majority also indicates that the principal sources of information (together with books and special studies) were social contacts, leisure time activities, and informal conversation.

On the other hand, Rose[5] has emphasized some of the difficulties that may develop if students or more senior scholars are expected to act as cross-national mediators when they feel themselves unprepared to perform that function. The report by Rose is entitled "Academic Sojourners," and deals with Senior Fulbright Programs in East Asia and the Pacific area. Over one hundred former Fulbright Scholars and a number of administrative officers of binational programs were interviewed, and mail surveys were conducted with a large sample of Fulbright alumni. There is a striking parallel between the problems raised in Rose's report and many of those previously dealt with in this volume.

The Executive Secretary of a binational commission is quoted as saying: "People to people understanding begins on a person to person basis. That is what this program is really all about."[6] The detailed interviews with individual scholars together with the questionnaires indicate that many of them accepted this goal as a valid one. Rose concludes that the "Fulbright Program in East Asia and the Pacific has well served its participants, <u>having clearly enhanced their mutual understanding</u> [emphasis supplied], their academic achievement and their personal honor. It has been a model for interpersonal, intercultural relations."[7]

One of his recommendations is very similar to what has been said above, namely, that "the roles and expectations of the various agencies of the exchange process be clarified, and common orientations be adopted."[8] Many grantees expressed a willingness to reach wider audiences and to serve as more effective "cultural interpreters," and it was suggested that "the use of senior grantees as 'Occasional Fulbright Scholars' should be more fully institutionalized in order to allow those willing to serve in such roles greater opportunities to do so."[9]

In the preceding chapter, we have presented and analyzed the results obtained in the area of national and ethnic relations. We turn now to a discussion of other consequences of the sojourn as seen by the participants themselves in a variety of areas. They were asked, for example, to indicate on a scale from "very satisfied" to "very dissatisfied" how they judged their experiences abroad. (See Table 3.5, Chapter 3.)

With regard to their overall experience, it is clear that for the foreign students in our investigation, satisfaction outweighed dissatisfaction in all countries. We base this general conclusion on the fact that in no country does the mean rating reach 3 ("neutral"), so that there can be no doubt that in all groups the students tend to rate their experiences as positive. There are of course variations among the countries which we included. Kenya ranks particularly high in all the average judgments made, with Brazil usually rather close behind, both with regard to academic and nonacademic experiences.

If we look at the percentages of those who were "very satisfied" or "satisfied" at the time we questioned them, we find that these include more than half of our sample in all countries, except in the case of Hong Kong and Iran as to satisfaction with the overall general and social (nonacademic) experience, and also Iran as to aspects other than studies.

We have always felt, on the basis of our own experience as well as what others have written about international educational exchange, that most participants are satisfied with their year abroad. (We questioned our foreign students toward the middle of the academic year, and our analysis of the interviews shows that the degree of satisfaction usually, though not always, increases before the end of the sojourn.) For this reason, we consider it important to look at the proportion of dissatisfied students, since it has been our hope that research in this area might identify some of the sources of dissatisfaction and thereby make a contribution to their reduction. Those who indicated that they were "very dissatisfied" are on the whole very rare; they exceed 5 percent with regard to "overall academic experience" only in Hong Kong; with regard to "general and social (nonacademic) experience" again in Hong Kong, but also in Iran and France; "with regard to studies" in no country; and with regard to "other aspects" of the experience in Iran, France, and India. If we combine the "dissatisfied" and "very dissatisfied" groups in order to obtain a general impression of the degree of dissatisfaction, the figures reach the substantial figure of 20 percent or more for "academic experience" in France and Hong Kong; for "general and social" experience in France, Hong Kong, India, and Japan; for "my studies" in no country; and for "other aspects" only in France. Almost no dissatisfaction is expressed by foreign students in Kenya.

The students were also asked to indicate to what extent they felt that they had changed; they ranked each item presented to them from very much (value of 1) to very little (value of 5) or none (value of 6). The results are presented in Table 7.1.

As far as "personal change" is concerned (again using the figure of 3 as the dividing line), it is immediately clear that there is very little change in "religious attitudes," although somewhat more in India than anywhere else. "Political opinions" also remain very stable in all countries, but a little less so than in the case of religion. In other areas, the reported changes are more substantial. The means remain below 3 (that is to say, there is considerable change) in the case of all countries for "personal development" except for Iran; for "intellectual development" also almost everywhere, again with Iran as the sole exception; for "self-confidence" in all countries except Hong Kong; and for feelings of "independence" everywhere. Once again, the situation in Kenya is particularly striking, since foreign students in that country report more change than anywhere else with regard to personal and intellectual development as well as in feelings of independence, and with regard to self-confidence are exceeded only in India, and then very slightly. (We shall return to the special case of Kenya below.)

There is overwhelming evidence to the effect that the foreign sojourn is seen as having opened up new research interests, ideas, or opportunities. The affirmative answer for this item exceeds 60 percent in the case of every country, ranging from a low of 68.5 percent in Iran to a high of 92.6 percent in the case of Brazil.

It is more difficult to summarize the results with regard to the impact on the students' views of their own country. In no case does the majority feel that they have developed more positive attitudes as a consequence of the stay at a foreign university; the range is from 31.5 percent in Iran and 32 percent in the United Kingdom

TABLE 7.1

Personal Change and Impact Perceived from the Sojourn

	Brazil	Canada	France	Hong Kong	India	Iran	Japan	Kenya	U.K.	U.S.	West Germany
As a result of your experience living in this country, how much have you changed in regard to the following areas:*											
Your personal development	2.347	2.247	2.383	2.375	2.643	3.179	2.103	1.553	2.316	2.407	2.526
Your intellectual development	2.218	2.242	2.400	2.700	2.125	3.044	2.433	1.723	2.386	2.366	2.487
Your political opinions	4.035	3.626	3.663	3.829	3.696	4.926	3.862	3.675	3.885	3.596	3.474
Your religious attitudes	4.518	4.669	4.979	4.850	3.232	5.235	4.793	4.783	4.978	4.628	4.342
Your feelings of self-confidence	2.718	2.757	2.846	3.049	2.054	2.986	2.643	2.205	2.909	2.881	2.868
Your feelings of independence	2.748	2.592	2.935	2.927	2.071	3.075	2.517	2.060	2.829	2.656	2.846

Has your experience
opened up new
research interests,
ideas, or oppor-
tunities for you?
(in percentages)

Yes	92.6	81.0	85.1	81.0	81.5	68.5	82.8	73.7	86.0	85.9	87.0
No	7.4	19.0	14.9	19.0	18.5	31.5	17.2	26.2	14.0	14.1	13.0

In what way has
your stay affected
your view of your
own country?
(in percentages)

I am more positive now about my country	42.8	33.1	40.2	41.7	32.7	31.5	43.3	49.0	32.0	36.0	47.0
No effect	53.8	53.5	44.6	27.8	52.7	60.3	50.0	46.0	49.0	53.3	41.0
I am more negative now about my country	3.4	13.5	15.2	30.6	14.5	8.2	6.7	5.0	19.0	10.7	12.0

*Means were calculated with "very much" (value of 1) through "very little" (value of 5) and "none" (value of 6) for individual country samples.

Source: Compiled by the authors.

93

to 49 percent in Kenya and 47 percent in Germany. More striking
are the variations in the development of more negative attitudes toward the home country, which may perhaps be considered as an unhappy and certainly undesired consequence. The figures remain
below 10 percent in the case of four countries (Brazil, Iran, Japan,
and Kenya), and rise above 20 percent only in the case of Hong Kong
(30.6 percent), although they are rather substantial in the United
Kingdom (19 percent). This represents a rather paradoxical situation, since those responsible for exchange programs are usually
desirous of developing friendly attitudes toward the host country,
but not at the expense of more negative feelings regarding a student's own country.

This is related to an item discussed earlier (Table 7.1). Students were asked to indicate whether, as the result of the foreign
sojourn, they would like to stay in the country in which they were
now studying, return home, go to another country, or had no preference in this respect. (The general issue of the "brain drain" has
already been discussed in Chapter 6.) In all countries, it is a minority of foreign students who express the desire to remain, but the proportion reaches 25.6 percent in Hong Kong, and varies from about
13 to 18 percent in most other countries. The lowest percentage in
this category is found in Kenya (10.7 percent) which is a somewhat
surprising result in view of the high degree of satisfaction expressed
by foreign students in that country, as indicated in those portions of
Table 4.5 discussed above. The proportion of foreign students in
Kenya who plan to return to their own country reaches the astonish-
ing figure of 81 percent, which is far out of line with the results obtained anywhere else. Those studying in Hong Kong are least enthusiastic about returning home (41 percent).

We shall attempt a further analysis of the national variations
in data reported in this chapter when we deal with the individual national profiles (Chapter 10). The results as a whole clearly indicate
a reasonably high degree of satisfaction in general as far as the individual students themselves are concerned. For those who have
had their foreign sojourn in the United States, a recent summary by
Flack, based on an extensive review and evaluation of published research since 1967, concludes as follows; ". . . the sojourn and educational experience tends to engender a more sophisticated, differ-
entiated, personalized and concretized knowledge and perception of
the host society, its achievements and problems, its peoples and
policies, and of its 'ways of life,' as compared to 'knowledge' and
images held before."[10] This is usually reflected in a reduction of
ethnocentric stereotypes, greater understanding of the functioning of
the host society, and a heightened awareness of its diversity. "The
result is a soberer appraisal of some of its features, values, and

practices and of their relevance to one's own role, one's field of activity, and one's own country." Our own results bear out these conclusions in the case of foreign students elsewhere as well.

THE RETROSPECTIVE STUDY

The reports by Hull and Lemke[11] and by Rose[12] dealing with Americans who have been abroad through the Fulbright-Hays Program, agree in their finding that most of the participants are happy about their experience, and are ready to urge others to follow their example. Our own results on the basis of answers obtained from scholars from 11 countries who have participated in the Fulbright or similar programs point in the same direction, in spite of substantial variations among countries in many respects. (See Table 7.2.) In our sample, most of the respondents were considered, or thought of themselves, as members of the teaching staff at the foreign institution, but those from Hong Kong and Canada were more likely to be students. The longest average stays abroad were found in those from Hong Kong (48 months) and Kenya (32 months), and the shortest (between 12 and 14 months) for scholars from Japan, India, and the United States. They varied also in the disciplines primarily involved: physical and biological sciences for those from the United Kingdom, Brazil, Iran, France, and Hong Kong; arts and humanities in the case of Japanese and Americans; behavioral and social sciences for those from Canada and India. Kenyans were divided between the humanities and the physical and biological sciences. These variations make the major agreements all the more striking. Difficulties were remembered, as was pointed out in Chapter 4, even after the passage of a considerable period of time, but the consensus was clearly that the experience had been worth while.

As for the more specific perceived consequences, it was almost universally agreed that the sojourn resulted in "stimulation to continue in one's academic field." There was a widespread feeling also that the experience abroad had "increased enjoyment in learning about other countries." For example, 87 percent of the Americans regarded this as an important consequence.

In every country, a majority of the respondents agreed that the foreign sojourn had a positive effect (either "definitely" or "somewhat") on their careers. This was the response of 100 percent of Kenyans, 95 percent Brazilians, 90 percent Hong Kong, 88.7 percent Iranians, 85.9 percent United States, 83.1 percent United Kingdom, 80 percent India, 79.9 percent France, 79.6 percent Canada, and 76.6 percent Japan.

TABLE 7.2

Consequences Attributed to the Sojourn: Rank* and Percent Response

Item	Canada	France	Hong Kong	India	Iran	Japan	Kenya	U.K.	U.S.	Brazil
Stimulation or motivation to continue in your field of choice	1 65%	1 71%	1 50%	1 68%	1 62%	1 80%		1 71%		1 23%
Increased enjoyment in learning about other countries	2 57%	2 62%				2 65%		2 65%	1 87%	2 18%
Becoming familiar with the actual professional standards applying within your field of specialization					2 61%					
Broadening your sensitivity to political aspects of life at home and abroad							1 80%		2 75%	

Realization of widely shared interests in your field of specialization	2 18%	2 70%		
Development of personal feelings of achievement and competence	1 80%		2 64%	
Opportunity to complete a phase of research or study while abroad		1 80%		2 44%

*Rank is based upon those respondents by country who reported that the consequence had been "very successfully" achieved "as a result of the educational experience abroad." Only those areas ranked 1 or 2 are reported here, and only those areas are listed which were ranked 1 or 2 by respondents in any single country sample.

Source: Compiled by the authors.

As far as advice to others is concerned, the range among those who said "Go!" was from 94 to 100 percent in all countries but one. The exception was Kenya, but even there the general response was definitely in the affirmative (75 percent). It is clear that in terms of personal satisfaction and a favorable judgment regarding the consequences of the foreign sojourn, the overwhelming reaction was positive.

THE INTERVIEWS

In the following chapter we shall turn more specifically to the interviews which were conducted with foreign students (on three separate occasions) and with more senior scholars. We shall limit ourselves at this point to one conclusion that emerges from the case studies of students, namely, that although a substantial number of them report serious difficulties at the beginning of the sojourn, they usually (although not always) handle them with reasonable success before the year is over. They do learn the local language, they find adequate housing, they make some friends, they learn the ropes at the university and in the society as a whole. In the large majority of cases, they end the year abroad feeling that it has indeed been worth while.

In an appendix to Hull's report of the results obtained in the United States, he and K. Finney present a number of case studies of individual foreign students. They conclude: "While there are coping and adjustment variables that individually influence the sojourn experiences of the foreign students in the United States, in general the sojourn itself is a period of intellectual and personal growth for the individuals in question. The educational sojourn is almost always reported to have been a healthy, worthwhile, and positive experience for the individual."[13]

The same may be said of the large majority of foreign students in all the countries included in our investigation.

NOTES

1. Otto Klineberg, International Educational Exchange (Paris: Mouton, 1976).

2. Ibid., p. 14.

3. Ingrid Eide, ed., Students as Links between Cultures (Oslo: Universitetsforlaget, 1970).

4. Ibid., p. 178.

5. Peter Q. Rose, "Academic Sojourners: A Report on The Senior Fulbright Programs in East Asia and the Pacific" (Washington, D.C.: Department of State, Bureau of Educational and Cultural Affairs, Office of Policy and Plans, 1976), and Peter Q. Rose, "The Senior Fulbright-Hays Program in East Asia and the Pacific," International Educational and Cultural Exchange 12, no. 2 (Fall 1976): 19-23.

6. Quoted in Rose, "Academic Sojourners," p. 34.

7. Rose, "Academic Sojourners," p. 2.

8. Ibid., p. 4.

9. Ibid., p. 9.

10. Michael J. Flack, "Results and Effects of Study Abroad," Annals of the American Academy of Political and Social Science 324 (1976): 111.

11. W. Frank Hull IV and Walter H. Lemke, Jr., "Retrospective Assessment of the United States Senior Fulbright-Hays Program," International Educational and Cultural Exchange 13, no. 2 (Spring 1978): 6-9.

12. Rose, "Academic Sojourners."

13. W. Frank Hull IV and Kevin P. Finney, "Longitudinal Case Studies of Foreign Students during Their Initial Educational Sojourn," in Hull, Foreign Students in the United States of America: Coping Behavior within the Educational Environment (New York: Praeger, 1978), p. 224.

8

THE PROCESS OF COPING:
AN ANALYSIS OF
THE CASE STUDIES

As has already been indicated, we conducted two varieties of interviews or "case studies" as part of our investigation. There was, on the one hand, a series of three interviews with a sample of foreign students at three stages—at the beginning, the middle, and toward the end of their academic year abroad; and on the other, a retrospective assessment by a sample of more senior respondents 10 to 15 years after their foreign sojourn. Although the statistical comparisons of the results obtained through the questionnaires may legitimately be regarded as the core of our investigation, and will undoubtedly inspire greater confidence because of the larger size of the samples, we felt that the interviews might also make a substantial contribution to our analysis.

More specifically, it was our hope that this contribution would be of value for the following reasons:

1. The questionnaires provided information about the foreign students at one particular moment in time, about midway through the academic year. The results obtained deal with the point reached in the coping process at that moment; they contain little information about how that point was arrived at, or about the final significance of the academic sojourn. We had the hope that the three successive interviews would add to our knowledge of the process as a whole, of the changes that occur as the students gradually come to grips with their problems. For certain issues, the attention paid to the whole process may be crucial—for example, in connection with the U-curve, which is discussed in the following chapter.

2. Secondly, we were convinced that a deeper understanding of the process of coping would be facilitated by the personal and friendly contact between the interviewer and the respondent. Many

of the reports received about the interviews do indeed indicate that good rapport was established, and that the situation encouraged freer expression of emotional reactions both with regard to the negative and the positive aspects of the experience. The interviewer was also able to ask additional questions which clarified some of the reactions obtained, as well as to "probe" for further details regarding the reasons for such reactions.

3. The long-range or retrospective interviews had to a considerable degree the same purpose, namely to put the respondents (in this case older individuals, many of them in responsible academic posts, and occasionally engaged in artistic activity or in governmental departments) at their ease, to establish rapport with them, and to give them in turn the possibility of asking questions of the interviewer regarding the purpose of the research enterprise. These particular interviews as well as the questionnaires directed to a larger sample of similar respondents, asked questions about a sojourn experienced 10 to 15 years earlier, and we have no certainty that the recollections reported are entirely accurate in detail. We have already made mention of the "sleeper effect," first identified by Hovland et al. in their study of attitudes and the extent to which attitudes may change a considerable time after exposure to an experience which is designed to produce such change but does not occur immediately after the experience. This may be due to further reflection, or to other reinforcing or even contradictory experiences. In our study, the time interval is much greater, but we were convinced that something could be learned by introducing the long-term perspective in the judgments made concerning the year abroad. There may also be a "halo effect," which adds a kind of rosy glow to what at the time might have been troublesome or tiring, but we have no way of demonstrating whether our data were influenced in this (or the opposite) direction.

4. One further reason for the interviews was our feeling that they might serve as a kind of test of the validity of our findings. By validity in this context we are referring to the practice of studying the same phenomenon by the use of two different techniques, on the assumption that if they agree, our conclusions may be presented with added confidence. The interviews may then serve not only as examples of our findings but also as further evidence that these findings are valid. Unfortunately we were not able to obtain interviews, either of foreign students or of senior scholars who had been abroad for a substantial period, from all the 11 countries in which our study was conducted. In some countries, our colleagues made a late start because arrangements we thought we had made for the collection of the case histories fell through, mainly because of difficulties in obtaining adequate financial support. It was only through

the kindness of those colleagues who took over the responsibility in spite of the lack of adequate time and resources, that we were able to obtain data. This delay did not prevent the successful application of the questionnaires, but in some cases it made it impossible to arrange for the interviews. Case studies of foreign students are, however, available from seven countries, namely Brazil, Canada, France, Hong Kong, India, Japan, and the United States. As for the restrospective interviews with the more senior scholars, material was obtained in France, Hong Kong, India, and the United States.

There is one further limitation that must be recognized. The three interviews with foreign students were designed to throw light on the changes that had occurred during the year abroad, and for this reason it was important to be able to compare what was said during the first, second, and third interviews respectively. Unfortunately, a number of interviewers did not keep this temporal distinction sufficiently in mind, presenting instead a general account of what the respondent reported about his experience without always making clear in what period of the year the particular event or situation occurred. We still feel that the interviews contain a great deal of relevant material.

Brief reference was made in Chapter 4 to what the interviews contain regarding the problems and difficulties encountered. We shall now consider this same area in somewhat greater detail, with emphasis on the complaints made and the specific ways in which they were expressed, and on how they changed in character and intensity as time progressed. Our approach will once again be chronological, beginning with the period that preceded the sojourn abroad, continuing through its various stages, and ending with the return home (or the failure to do so).

THE PROBLEM OF SELECTION

In Chapter 1, reference was made to the rather haphazard manner in which students are selected, or select themselves, for a sojourn at a foreign university. The issue of selection did not enter directly into our research design, since we started out with foreign students who were already abroad. In the interviews, however, it was usually possible to obtain relevant information at least indirectly, since many of the students indicated the factors that had led to the decision to go. Foreign students who were interviewed in France, for example, were there for a rather large variety of reasons. Some came because of a general admiration for French culture; others, because they were working in some area of French

literature or history; some were eager to study under a particular
professor of whom they had heard, or because scholarships were
available which they accepted although they would have preferred
to go elsewhere; a few came at the insistence of their parents.
Selection is indeed a varied and uncertain process as far as these
students are concerned.

The following excerpts from the interviews conducted in
France illustrate these variations. A Polish student of economics
came to do research for his doctoral dissertation and to become
familiar with French cultural life. A Yugoslav interested in paint-
ing wished to study art and "all other expressions of cultural life
which he was sure to find in France." A Japanese came to Paris
for two years "to do research in French literature and to improve
her French." A young Iranian woman "came to study sociology in
Paris because her brother had studied here." A German medical
student wished to get training in a French medical faculty and to
learn about the organization of French hospitals. An Algerian
"wanted to go to England, but as it was easier to obtain a French
scholarship, he accepted it as a second choice." An American girl
came to study French literature. A young Iranian geologist was
sent by his company to specialize in oil geology in a French research
institute. A Yugoslav came to Paris, which his countrymen consider
to be "the center of the world." A political science student from
Ghana "wants to get to know the life of the French people and their
political views, particularly concerning Africa." A Greek from
Lebanon came because the situation in that country made university
studies difficult, but also because his parents insisted that he do so.
A student from Zaire was sent to France by his government; one
from Mauritius chose France because "it was the best scholarship
he could obtain."

The reasons given by foreign students in other countries are
substantially similar, but other factors may occasionally enter.
One Iranian student in Canada wished "to get away from an unpleasant political situation" in his own country. An Egyptian gave the
same reason for leaving Egypt, in addition to the desire "to avoid
conscription in the Egyptian army." A Peruvian "did not choose
the Canadian university himself but was forced to come here by his
father." An Indian student came to the United States because "a
degree earned at an American university is accepted all over the
world," but another student from the same country wanted to study
in England, and came to the United States "by default." One from
Taiwan would have preferred to go to West Germany, but found it
easier to obtain an American visa. One from Ghana wished to obtain a "premium education" that he could apply to his country's
development.

These personal accounts of the reasons for study abroad represent only one aspect of the problem of selection, namely, the conscious or admitted motivations. The other aspect, at least as important, refers to the manner in which the students are selected, or in other words, to whether they are qualified to go. When fellowships are granted, it may be expected that the institutions responsible (the United Nations and its agencies, governments, foundations, and so on) do a certain amount of screening, since obviously not all applicants are successful in obtaining the available financial grants, but even in such cases the selection process is usually restricted to a judgment of academic competence and rarely extends to the attributes of personality which may also contribute to success or failure respectively.

PREPARATION FOR THE SOJOURN ABROAD

There are a number of ways in which students may prepare themselves for the stay at a foreign university; most obvious is the need to make sure that they have an adequate knowledge of the language of the country to which they go. This topic has already been discussed in Chapter 4 on the basis of results obtained from our total sample, but the interviews give us some additional details and permit judgments by the interviewer regarding the extent of the language difficulties of the students concerned. These difficulties are indeed more serious than we had anticipated.

To start again with foreign students interviewed in France, we were startled to discover that a substantial minority (12 out of 28) could not speak French enough to answer relatively simple questions in that language on the occasion of the first interview. * As indicated above, most of the students were able to handle French reasonably well by the time of their third interview, but by then a great deal of valuable time had been lost. Not surprisingly, many of these students urged better language preparation before departure. They also suggested, in a number of cases, that a one-year stay at a foreign university was not sufficient, mainly because so much time elapsed before they really felt at home in French.

Difficulties with language emerge in the interviews with foreign students in other countries, on the whole similar in extent and in frequency to the findings in France. We were particularly struck

---

*Fortunately, we had a polyglot interviewer, Henryka Glogowski, who was able to conduct the first interview either in French, English, German, Polish, Portuguese, or Spanish.

by the language difficulties reported by the students in Hong Kong, where both English and Mandarin are required at the university, as well as Cantonese for meaningful contact with the local population. We had learned in our earlier study[1] that language constituted an especially difficult problem for foreign students in Japan. It was more surprising to discover how many foreign students had problems in Brazil, in spite of the general similarity between Spanish (since most of them came from other Latin American countries) and Portuguese, partly because of local variations in accent. In their case, however, the difficulty was usually very quickly overcome.

The interviews occasionally yield interesting information regarding variations in linguistic standards for admission in different countries or universities. One Iranian student, for example, interviewed at a western university in the United States, reported that he had been in England in order to study economic development, but the faculty there "demanded a high degree of fluency in English from the students; consequently, he was required to spend one year studying English before he could properly enroll in the program. Faced with such an alternative, he decided to terminate his study there and come to the United States instead." There, too, he was urged to take additional courses in English, but he was also admitted to the required courses in economics. His performance was so poor that he was informed at the end of the first quarter that he would have to take a leave of absence "to improve his English before he could continue with his program in economics." Evidently, the American university was somewhat more lenient, but this turned out not to be particularly helpful. We had previously been informed by British colleagues in our first study that their universities were very strict with regard to language competence.

There are other aspects of advance preparation that may also have important practical implications. There are, for example, great variations in the structure, calendar, course requirements, instructional content, and relations with the teaching staff at different universities. Such variations occur among universities even within the same country, and are all the more striking when different countries are concerned. Many of our respondents complained about the lack of information regarding the foreign university, or about the new culture, received in advance of their arrival. A Panamanian male student in Brazil states that "he was well informed before coming as to the new university, but had insufficient information regarding the life outside the university." Another student, from El Salvador, regarded his advance knowledge of the courses and subject matter as insufficient. An American arrived in Brazil without knowledge of bureaucratic and administrative

complexities, "advantages and opportunities offered to students,"
how to obtain documents, how to use the libraries. A girl from
Panama found the advance information insufficient, and urges "the
establishment of an information center for foreign students in
Brazil." An American male studying in Japan complained of "difficulty getting to know the details of study-abroad programs," and
feels that although the institutions in which he was enrolled in the
United States have program offices, "they are not functioning
properly." He believed that "good orientation" regarding "manners
and customs, climate, social systems" is definitely needed before
a student travels to a foreign country. There can be no doubt that
many students would have been less disturbed on arrival if there
had been better advance warning as to what they might expect. An
American girl in France urged that adequate advance preparation be
given regarding everyday life in a large city, local customs, and
the educational system. We shall return later to this aspect of the
foreign sojourn; it appears to us to be of major importance.

FIRST EXPERIENCES AT THE FOREIGN UNIVERSITY

What has been said above about lack of advance information
will obviously have relevance to the first contacts with the new university, since uncertainty as to the rules and regulations may result in all sorts of bureaucratic entanglements. Sometimes the
needed information can be readily obtained after arrival. The
American student in Japan referred to above found the "orientation
and guidance" available at his new university "very helpful and very
much appreciated." Another American, in Hong Kong, found the
information he had received before arrival to be incorrect, and that
the orientation program at the university was definitely helpful.
Sometimes this is made available indirectly, as in the case of a
Canadian girl who received no orientation at the university in Hong
Kong but met a student who had been in Canada and helpfully introduced her to campus life. The general impression we get from the
interviews is that lack of knowledge as to how to proceed during the
first days at the new institution is fairly widespread and is found in
all countries. The difficulty is usually overcome rather rapidly,
but not always. Most universities do have an orientation program,
and they often have foreign student advisers. Strangely enough,
however, some of the students we interviewed did not know of the
existence of the advisers nor how to get in touch with them.

More disturbing is the problem of being admitted to the academic program of one's choice, and at the level which previous
training would seem to the students to be justified. This combined

issue of admission and of "equivalences" or "credits" may undoubtedly cause great anxiety and frustration. One male student from
El Salvador went to Brazil expecting to study medicine, believing
he had been admitted to the Medical School, only to find on arrival
that he had been assigned to the School of Nursing. At the time of
his third interview, he was still waiting to be transferred. This is
undoubtedly an extreme case, but the kind of problem it raises is by
no means rare. There have been attempts to improve the situation
in some areas; for example, French and West German university
authorities have established a set of equivalences which may in
time take care of this issue as far as these two countries are concerned. On the other hand, West German students usually do not
know until their return home how much their foreign study will
"count" toward the diploma or degree for which they are working.
This whole issue of equivalences is exceedingly complicated since
university systems differ so markedly that it is often difficult if not
impossible to evaluate what has been done elsewhere, both in terms
of the general content of the instruction and also its quality. It has
been suggested that as far as degrees or diplomas are concerned,
it should be possible to reach international agreement, and the paper
or parchment which the student receives should then be recognized
everywhere in the world. This is certainly difficult if not impossible to realize under present conditions.

THE ACADEMIC EXPERIENCE

It is clear that the issues already raised in this chapter—selection, preparation, language facility—will exert an important
influence on the actual sojourn at a foreign university. The aspects
to which we now turn are therefore not independent of what has already been said. As a matter of fact, the chronological presentation we are using here is in some respects artificial, since every
stage or aspect of the sojourn is related to all the others. This
will become clearer in Chapter 11, which deals more directly with
these interrelationships. We still regard it as useful to present
successively some of our findings with regard to the various aspects
of the sojourn abroad.

In one sense, the present topic may be regarded as central to
the whole experience. The actual work at the university, including
the courses taken, success or failure in fulfilling the requirements,
relations with the academic staff, degree of satisfaction with the
quality of the teaching, may be regarded as the crucial issue of our
investigation, and the attitude of the foreign students toward the
instruction they are receiving is the key to the success of the whole

enterprise. We have already seen (Chapter 7) that our statistical data indicate that most foreign students do judge their teachers favorably as far as the quality of instruction is concerned. The interviews in general support this impression, and as a consequence they may be considered as offering further confirmation of the conclusions reached in Chapter 7.

We did not obtain direct data regarding the actual success or failure of foreign students in passing their courses or otherwise reaching the goals (diploma, degree, certificate) which they had set themselves on arrival. Previous investigations on this aspect are somewhat contradictory. In Eide's study, 88 percent of the Egyptian students and 97 percent of the Iranians obtained a degree from the host country before they went home.[2] The figure dropped to 71 percent in the case of the Indians, but this is interpreted as due to the level of education the students had achieved before leaving home. An earlier study in Germany by Aich,[3] however, reported that about 80 percent of Asian and African students fail in intermediate, and 40 percent fail in final examinations. This high proportion of failures may be due, in Aich's opinion, to the fact that these foreign students have limited qualifications, since many of them came to Germany because they could not gain admission to universities in their own country. More recent information reported by Von Alemann[4] indicates that Aich's data may not be typical, since results obtained in 1968 and 1969 show that German and foreign students differ only very slightly as far as general success or failure in examinations is concerned. Bochner[5] makes a similar point with regard to foreign students in Australia. Kapur[6] found a higher failure or drop-out rate ("wastage") among foreign than among British students at the University of Edinburgh, but at the University of Sussex, the failure rate among foreign students is low, probably because of the careful selection process and the guidance supplied by university tutors. It is difficult to draw definite conclusions from this scattered evidence, but it is probable that the failure rate is indeed a little higher among foreign students.

Our own inquiry, particularly as far as the interviews were concerned, placed the accent on how the students felt about the academic experience, how satisfied they were with the instruction received. As indicated above, the usual reaction to our questions in this connection was positive. In Canada, a girl from the Bahamas said she "felt satisfied with her academic experience"; so did a female student from Venezuela. On the other hand, an Italian girl had some difficulties in her courses; a boy from Peru complained that "the university administration (including secretaries) had lied to him and given him a 'run around' when he first arrived"; another, from Iran, stated that he was not given enough information regarding progress in his studies; a girl from Singapore had difficulty "with her courses and with the administration." In India, a male student from Afghanistan is described as "extremely happy with his experience; at times he sounds too happy and contented with what he receives in the form of education." A student from Mauritius, however, gradually becomes dissatisfied with his academic experience. An American student in Hong Kong felt "that the teachers were very helpful, most of them provided intellectual stimulation, their teaching quality was good"; a Canadian girl thought that some of her teachers were good, others unsatisfactory; a Japanese boy was grateful that his teachers were accessible; a Chinese from Singapore said that "there was sufficient intellectual stimulation"; one from Malaysia, however, "was quite disappointed with some of the instructors, who merely repeated facts and concepts from the texts."

There were two specific complaints raised with some frequency, one by foreign students in the United States, the second in France. A large number of American universities have introduced the term system, which involves breaking up the academic year into relatively brief segments (ten weeks or so) which constitute independent units of instruction followed by examinations at the end of each term. For a Canadian, "his one source of academic dissatisfaction was the term system and the heavy pressures associated with it"; a Thai girl spoke of "the rigors of the term system"; one from Taiwan felt that "the 10-week term placed undue pressure on her." This complaint recurs with (to us) surprising frequency. Although every university has the right to choose whatever yearly calendar appears to be the most satisfactory, it might perhaps be possible to inform foreign students more clearly as to what to expect, so that the need to prepare for examinations at brief intervals will not come as such a disturbing surprise.

The problem faced by foreign students in France is quite different, and relates to the difficulties encountered by those who wish to make contact with their professors, and to discuss their studies with them. A student from Ghana is satisfied with his lectures, "but the teachers are inaccessible after classes, and one doesn't get informed about the progress one is making in the studies"; for a Lebanese student, "the teachers are not easily accessible"; for a student from Zaire, the "general atmosphere is formal and impersonal." This is obviously a situation which French students face in the same manner and to the same degree as do those from other countries. One of the authors of this report has been stationed in Paris since 1962. When he first arrived, he received information regarding his courses and seminars, and he then asked, "What about office hours?" The answer he received was, "Office hours! You have no office!" It was only three years later, when a research center was organized under his direction, that he was given an office in which he could receive his students. The late Kurt Lewin, a distinguished social psychologist who left Germany for the United States, once remarked that the major difference between European and American universities was that the doors to the offices of American professors were always open! The present investigation indicates that this is true in many other countries as well—but not in France.

Apart from these two examples—the term system in the United States and the "mandarinat" in France—most foreign students expressed themselves as being satisfied with the instruction they were receiving.

ADAPTATION TO SOCIETY IN GENERAL

When we turn to the experience with society as a whole, and specifically to life outside the university, we are struck once again by the manner in which the interviews, in addition to our statistical data, reveal the interrelations among the factors analyzed. Language facility is of obvious importance within the university, and it is frequently mentioned as having major implications outside as well. Students usually seek contact with the general population and not only with other students, and the lack of linguistic competence is frequently mentioned as a handicap in that connection. In two of the countries in our study, this issue took on a special form. In Canada, for example, the foreign students attended an English-speaking university in the city of Montreal, and obviously they had to be competent in English. What they did not always realize in advance, however, was that the majority of the population in that city is French-speaking, and that they had to learn French as well if they wished to establish contact. Since the situation is at present complicated by the insistence of many French-Canadians to use only French, the foreigners found that unless they spoke that language they were often ignored. A number of them speak of "discrimination" against them, and develop feelings of hostility against French-Canadians as a consequence. The second case of unexpected difficulty is that of Hong Kong. In the university, English is the major language of instruction, but courses in Mandarin are also given, and the foreign students had to learn that language as well. The general population, however, speaks Cantonese, and contacts were limited unless the students mastered that Chinese language as well; frustration occurred with some frequency.

There were a number of complaints regarding living conditions which had consequences both within and outside the university. These included finances in general, the special case of housing, the distance between lodgings and the university, transportation, food, climate. For these issues, important as they are, the interviews confirm the fact that they may indeed be troublesome, but that they are usually solved with reasonable success before the end of the sojourn. They are, however, all related to an issue of fundamental importance, namely, contact with the host population; this has been recognized in the existing literature, and is confirmed in our own findings (see especially Chapters 4, 5, and 6). The interviews provide further detail, often of a more personal nature, in this connection.

In Brazil, the interviews in general indicate relatively good relations between the foreign students (predominantly Latin American) and the local population. There are, however, exceptions. One girl from Peru disliked the "agitated life" in a large Brazilian city, and found the people "cold and unbalanced." A Bolivian male reported "little contact with Brazilians outside the university" during the first few months of his sojourn. A female student, also from Bolivia, stated that she is "too much alone." In Hong Kong, contacts in and outside the university were usually satisfactory, but one Japanese male reported that throughout the year his "circle of friends was mainly Japanese"; a Chinese male from Singapore found the relationship "with neighbors and others very superficial"; a Canadian female felt that "her contacts with the Chinese people were less frequent than she wished." The problem of contact is rarely raised in India, but one male student from Afghanistan complained that the "not too helpful nature of the local people has caused him a lot of annoyance"; one from Mauritius felt that "Indian friends have proved unfriendly, proud and money-minded."

In Canada, difficulty in making contact with the local population (complicated by the language problem to which reference was made above) occurred with some frequency. An Egyptian male reported that "his main problem seemed to be his lack of contact with people and resulting loneliness"; an Iranian also "felt he had a lack of contact with local people"; a Frenchman found it "hard to make more than superficial friendships"; a girl from the Bahamas "felt she had little contact with local people."

The "superficiality" of contacts or friendships mentioned by one foreign student in Canada recurs with some frequency in the references to contact with Americans. A West German male said he was meeting many Americans, but "the contacts were not deep enough"; an Indian male looked unsuccessfully for a "deep friendship with an American, someone with whom he could share personal feelings and be very open"; on the other hand, a student from Scotland started out with an initial impression of "superficiality" in relations with Americans but gradually changed his opinion as he "got to know some people more deeply."

To the extent that friendship on the part of Americans is considered, although by a minority, to be superficial, we may be dealing here with a stereotype which is expressed with some frequency particularly in Europe; this is to the effect that it is easy to "make friends" in the United States, but difficult to "make good friends." Whether this is true or not is hard to determine. It seems highly probable that a contributing factor may be a failure to understand certain cues in the cross-cultural contacts involved. Americans, for example, are almost certainly ready to call one another by their first names more quickly than are most other nationalities, and they will usually extend this habit to their relations with foreigners. The latter, much less likely to do so until an intimate relation has been established, may interpret being called by their first name as a sign that they have been accepted on a basis of real intimacy. When they discover that this is not the case, they may experience a feeling of disillusionment, and the conviction that "friendship" in the United States remains at an artificial level.

In France, the situation is very different. A large majority of the foreign students interviewed came to that country expecting not only an excellent academic and cultural experience, but also one rich in personal and social relations as well. In general, they were disappointed in this latter connection. A somewhat smaller number, but still a majority, felt lost and lonely at the beginning of the sojourn, made some efforts at becoming accepted by local students and the community, but found this so difficult that they ended up limiting their relationships to their own fellow-nationals or to other foreign students and non-students. One of the reasons for the difficulty encountered may be the fact that being invited into a French home still involves in most cases more elaborate preparations on the part of the hosts and more concern to serve a meal rich both in quality and quantity, than would be the case in most other countries. In any event, the results obtained in our interviews confirm those found through the application of the questionnaire; foreign students in France complained of the lack of personal contacts more than did those in all the other countries included in our study.

Other social factors mentioned by some of our respondents included boy-girl relations, the pros and cons of dormitory life as compared to sojourn with a local family, the use of sports as a means of making contacts, the role of the university and of the foreign student adviser in helping to establish such contacts, and the need to avoid artificiality in arranging for international meetings under university auspices. There was in addition the question of

ethnic (or "racial") prejudice and discrimination, and also the effect of the sojourn on the attitude toward the host country. With
regard to the latter two items, the interviews added little to the
results obtained on the larger sample and reported on in Chapter 6,
but they raise certain issues which require at least a brief mention.

The foreign students in general do not indicate that a great
deal of discrimination is directed against them. There was only
one such report in India, and very few in other countries. On the
other hand, there were a number of students who denied that they
were themselves discriminated against, but who said they had seen
or been told of discrimination directed at others, often their friends
or relatives. It is difficult to know how much weight to attach to
these indirect or vicarious experiences. They may be genuine, but
they may also be merely the expectation of what one should find on
the basis of current stereotypes. The same issue has previously
been raised by other investigators. In the study by Useem and
Useem[7] of Indian students who had been in the United Kingdom or
the United States, it was found that fewer than one-fourth had been
the objects of discrimination themselves, but more than three-
fourths "knew" of discrimination against others and were upset by
it. This raises the important issue as to the extent to which discrimination may be allied to what psychologists identify as "plural-
istic ignorance," in which all the members of a particular group
express one view while being certain that all the others in the group
would disagree. (The members of a college fraternity, for example, may all state their willingness to accept blacks or Jews while
attributing to all other members an unwillingness to do so.) Without, of course, denying the reality of discrimination, which may
affect housing and jobs as well as personal contacts in general, it
would be important to determine how much of it is real, and how
much imagined. The interviews reveal a greater frequency of discrimination noted in France than in the other countries in our study,
and affect particularly students of black African and Arab origin.
The numbers are too small, however, to permit us to attach great
importance to this finding.

One of the goals of international exchanges, as previously
noted, is that of fostering understanding and friendship among the
peoples concerned. As Flack has indicated in the case of foreign
students in the United States, the "realm of international relations
is probably the most difficult and most complex of the effect areas
considered. Seldom . . . was 'international understanding' opera-
tionally defined and then tested and followed up in action."[8] He goes
on to say that although the attitudes toward the whole experience
abroad were on the whole positive, and Americans were generally
liked, there was frequent criticism of specific United States foreign

policies and of aspects of the society, such as discrimination, the level of cultural life, ignorance of other societies, and so forth.

A note of uncertainty is also sounded by Wicks and Bochner, who write with regard to the presence of foreign students in Australia: "Whether Australia has attracted much international goodwill by providing places for students from other countries is an open question, since evidence on this issue is scarce indeed."[9]

Our own results in connection with this issue have already been reported in Chapter 6, but one aspect requires an additional comment on the basis of the interviews. We have the impression that in the majority of cases, foreign students do end their year with more favorable attitudes toward their hosts than when they started, but that the minority remaining unchanged or becoming more unfavorable is sufficiently large to warn those who administer these programs against excessive confidence in the outcome as far as international relations are concerned.

In the case of France in particular, our interviews present us with an interesting and striking paradox. A substantial majority in our sample (19 students out of 28) end up disliking the French and loving France. They find the country beautiful and interesting, and cities like Paris or Nice rich in culture and in academic opportunities. They would like to come back! For the French people, on the other hand, they use terms such as cold, rigid, selfish, self-centered, unsociable, convinced of their own superiority, failing in their obligations as hosts, xenophobic, and even racist. A minority consider them to be intelligent, helpful, polite, excellent company, and good friends. It is difficult to decide which of these attitudes, toward the country or the people, is more important or will have a more lasting effect. In any case, our sample is very small.

We shall limit ourselves to one further finding which illustrates the value of having interviews conducted at three successive stages during the foreign sojourn. Problems and difficulties do tend to become reduced with time—not always, but usually. A few examples indicate the nature of this tendency. An Indian male student at an American university stated during his first interview that he would have preferred to go to England. He thought it would be hard for him to adjust to the local life and social values. "People seemed less sincere about friendship, religion and life in general." He was afraid this would frustrate him. In the second interview, he indicated dissatisfaction with the intellectual stimulation. He has made a number of American friends, but nothing he views as a long-term stable friendship. By the third interview, he has what he considers good friends. He is satisfied in general with his life in the United States; he believes it has been a meaningful year for him, even though he feels that the department in which he works could be improved. A Panamanian male student in Brazil suffers at first from homesickness, has difficulty with the language and with his studies, finds his professors uncooperative, and has problems in obtaining the information he requires. He has definitely developed a more favorable attitude at the time of his second interview; he speaks the language better and has more frequent contact with Brazilians. At the third interview, he is described as "perfectly well adapted," and is about to terminate the academic year success-fully, having overcome all the difficulties mentioned at the beginning of his sojourn. Even when the outcome is less than perfectly satis-factory, the changes noted may be of interest. A male student from Zaire in France, for example, started out with difficulties in both the academic and social areas. The latter persisted through-out the year, but academically he states that he profits a great deal and he is very satisfied in spite of all the earlier difficulties.

Our general conclusion from an examination of the interviews is that a single interview, at any point of the sojourn, may be mis-leading. If it is conducted early in the year, it may place undue emphasis on problems and difficulties. If conducted at the end of the academic year, the interview may give the impression that things are going well, and that the difficulties are unimportant, whereas they may have been very distressing, and in any case they were responsible for loss of valuable time; also, if we learn more about them, we may be more successful in reducing their severity. The three successive interviews are therefore of value, although they require much more careful planning, and the necessary ar-rangements are much more complicated.

THE RETROSPECTIVE INTERVIEWS

As has already been indicated on the basis of the statistical analysis of the results obtained through the application of the ques-tionnaire, a very large proportion of the more senior scholars are glad they went abroad, and are prepared to recommend a similar experience to their friends and colleagues. This is not entirely due to the rosy glow which comes with the passage of time, since the interviews indicate that our respondents have not forgotten the problems they encountered. The generally positive outcome is emphasized in spite of the difficulties remembered.

The 18 Indian scholars who had been abroad occasionally, mentioned a number of problems which rarely appeared in the inter-views in other countries. With some frequency, those who went to the United States or to the United Kingdom complained of the attitude in the host country toward scholars from the Third World. One stated that "the faculty assumes ignorance in scholars from developing countries and consequently assumes exaggerated professional superiority." Another student felt that "the attitude of British university teachers is too patronizing and this is difficult to take for the senior scholars from India." It is of course hard to determine whether this was due to prejudice or to poorer training. In any case, it was a minority view. Another complaint referred to the fact that on the return home it was sometimes difficult to find a job in which the training obtained abroad might be put to good use. In other cases (and this was also reported by some of the scholars from Hong Kong), the job was a good one but local conditions (in agriculture, hospitals, social service) were such as to make the specific application of the newly acquired techniques difficult if not impossible. Several of the Indians also stressed the importance of better briefing, regarding both the university and the society, before departure. A small number said they experienced discrimination while abroad.

Those who went from Hong Kong (12 interviews), usually to the United Kingdom, reported a great deal of satisfaction and few difficulties. There was almost no instance of reported discrimination. The only major frustration was the difficulty of applying at home what was learned abroad. One scholar put it optimistically: "Although what I have learned is not useful in Hong Kong, I strongly feel that the time will come when they will need my assistance." One scholar who went to New Zealand had trouble at first with the local slang, and one who was in Japan required almost three years to overcome her language difficulty for academic as well as social purposes, but in Hong Kong this female dentist has many Japanese patients, and feels that it was worth while. The Hong Kong scholars in general urge more pre-departure orientation, and also recommend that those selected for a foreign sojourn should be mature and independent. The American sample all spoke of their sojourn abroad with enthusiasm.

The French scholars interviewed (20 cases) were almost uniformly enthusiastic about their foreign sojourn, a large majority reporting that it was a very positive, although sometimes indirect, factor in their professional advancement. A minority had language problems at first, and a very small minority had difficulty in establishing friendly contacts with the host population. On the other hand, slightly more than half said they knew very little about the foreign country on arrival, and urge a fuller orientation program. Almost all regarded their sojourn abroad as directly or indirectly a positive factor in their subsequent careers, and also as responsible for important personal development; at least half remain in contact, professional or friendly or both, with former teachers and fellow students all over the world. A large number comment on the informal atmosphere at the foreign universities and the accessibility of professors—which they contrast with the rigidity and formality of the French system. In general, they think that French scholars should go abroad in order to become more tolerant and receptive to new intellectual ideas, more open to human contacts, and less prejudiced. They also stress the importance of maturity in those who travel. Since there is less difference in scientific areas between France and other industrialized countries today than 15 to 20 years ago, their feeling is that a foreign sojourn is now less important academically than in relation to human and social development.

In spite of the almost universal enthusiasm for the sojourn abroad expressed in these retrospective interviews, there are also a number of specific practical suggestions for improvement. We shall return to these in Chapter 13.

NOTES

1. Otto Klineberg, International Educational Exchange (Paris: Mouton, 1976).

2. Ingrid Eide, editor, Students as Links between Cultures (Oslo: Universitetsforlaget, 1970).

3. P. Aich, Farbige unter Weissen (Cologne: Kiepenheuer and Witsch, 1962).

4. Klineberg, op. cit.

5. Stephen Bochner and P. Wicks, editors, Overseas Students in Australia (Sydney: New South Wales University Press, 1972).

6. R. L. Kapur, "Student Wastage at Edinburgh University," Edinburgh University Quarterly (1972): 353-77.

7. John Useem and Ruth H. Useem, The Western-Educated Man in India (New York: Dryden, 1955).

8. Michael J. Flack, "Results and Effects of Study Abroad," Annals of the American Academy of Political and Social Science 324 (1976): 115.

9. P. Wicks and S. Bochner, "A Continuing Inquiry," in Overseas Students in Australia, ed. S. Bochner and P. Wicks, op. cit., p. 228.

9

THE "U-CURVE" HYPOTHESIS:
OCCASIONAL OR UNIVERSAL?

Undoubtedly the best known and most widely recognized hypothesis relating to the adjustment of students to a sojourn culture within an educational environment is that known as the "U-curve." Posited by Sverre Lysgaard after studying 200 Norwegian Fulbright grantees who had received travel grants for various purposes and periods of time in the United States and who had returned to Norway by March 1953, the hypothesis states that:

> Adjustment as a process over time seems to follow a
> U-shaped curve: adjustment is felt to be easy and suc-
> cessful to begin with; then follows a "crisis" in which
> one feels less well adjusted, somewhat lonely and un-
> happy; finally one begins to feel better adjusted again,
> becoming more integrated into the foreign community.
> Or, to put it differently, we suggested that adjustment
> as a process over time operates at increasingly more
> intimate levels of contact with the community visited.
> The need for more intimate contact, however, makes
> itself felt before one is able to achieve such contact
> and for some time, therefore, one may feel "lonely"
> and maladjusted. [1]

It is important to look carefully at this hypothesis as well as how Sverre Lysgaard arrived at it before we study the present data with a view to its confirmation.

First of all, the hypothesis came about during a study of Norwegian Fulbright grantees to the United States. Second, data contributing to the hypothesis came from interviews, averaging an hour

and a half, with returning Fulbrighters in Oslo. Lysgaard noticed
in reviewing the interviews, that the adjustment of those Fulbrighters who had been in the United States less than 6 months or more
than 18 months tended to be "good." However, those who had been
in the United States between 6 and 18 months seemed to have ad-
justed to the United States "less well." Thus the adjustment curve
was based upon the following breakdowns by duration of sojourn:
(1) 6 months or less, (2) 6 to 18 months, and (3) more than 18
months.

The hypothesis has been revised by others, but only slightly.[2]
The main revisions have concerned the periods used for breaking
down the sojourn. For example, Richard T. Morris has suggested
that the period between the tenth and nineteenth months is the most
difficult one in foreign student adjustment.[3] George V. Coelho has
indicated that this period might really be from three months to
three years![4] In general, however, the hypothesis still stands:
adjustment follows a "U-shaped" curve with a period of frustration,
depression, or anxiety in the middle of the sojourn experience.

As was discussed in the volume presenting the U.S. data for
this present investigation,[5] there are methodological problems that
make it uniquely difficult to conduct research into the operation of
the "U-curve" hypothesis on a worldwide basis. While a great deal
of this type of research has been conducted on foreign students in
the United States and in Western Europe, it is unclear as to what effect the traditional "Christmas holidays" have on the operation of
the "U-curve." This appears to be a "down" period in foreign student adjustment, but it is also a depressing time for many natives
as well.

No one has yet shown that foreign students arriving in the
spring or winter go through identical ups and downs in adjustment.
Even if this were so, the reason for it may be that in Western universities the social patterns of students are generally set during
the fall, when all students are arriving for the first time or are returning, usually to new residences, and so forth; it may well be
that any new students entering into campus environments where
social patterns have already been established, will have difficulty
in fitting in and adjusting.

Most of the research has also been conducted by taking a
population of foreign students and looking at their attitudes and relationships, and so on, at one point in time on a pen and paper instrument. This approach obviously misses the progression of ups
and downs, if they do occur, within the process of adjustment of individual students to the host university. It is for this reason that
the present investigation has specifically conducted its research in
two ways: first, it will be recalled, samples of foreign students

were asked to complete the instruments midway in the academic year. If the "U-curve" hypothesis is valid, our data should indicate how the country samples of students view themselves during a supposedly "down" period, in contrast to an "up" period, in their adjustment. Second, random samples of newly arrived, nonimmigrant foreign students were interviewed and followed over the course of the initial academic year through case studies.

Certainly there should be an indication of the "U-curve" pattern of adjustment in these more clinical samples over that academic year in each country. There are, to summarize, two distinct types of data that need to be considered for this present discussion: the statistical data collected midway in the academic year as well as the longitudinal interview data collected throughout the initial year from the samples of newly arrived foreign students in each participating country.

INTERNATIONAL STATISTICAL DATA

As was indicated in Chapter 3 (Table 3.1), in all of the study country samples the largest number of respondents had been in the sojourn countries for more than two years. This was true everywhere except in Hong Kong and in Kenya, where the largest number had been in those respective countries from five to eight months. Because of the point in the academic year at which the data were collected, the samples naturally peaked at the five to eight-month period as well as at the 13 to 18-month period in most countries. It is also important to recall that the average age of the respondents in the samples ranged from 22.9 years in India to 27.0 years in Japan. In other words, the present international samples are evidently younger than Lysgaard's Fulbrighters and they had been in the host country for a longer period of time.

The data from the various country samples were studied through the following analyses:

1. Cross tabulations: 4 months and less compared with more than 2-year duration (Chapter Appendix A).
2. Cross tabulations: 4 months and less compared with 9 to 12 months (Chapter Appendix B).
3. Cross tabulations: under 1 month compared with 1 to 4 months compared with 5 to 8 months compared with 9 to 12 months compared with 13 to 18 months compared with 19 to 24 months compared with more than 2 years (Chapter Appendix C).
4. Cross tabulations: 4 months and less compared with 5 to 24 months compared with more than 2 years (Chapter Appendix D).

5. Cross tabulations: 4 months and less compared with 5 to 8 months compared with 9 to 12 months (Chapter Appendix E).

The various groupings by duration of sojourn were analyzed because of the disagreement in previous research and discussions as to the particular time periods most likely to evidence a "U-curve" phenomenon.

If the "U-curve" hypothesis is operating internationally in our data, crucial variables should display no significant differences between more recent and more long-term sojourners on the basis of Analyses 1 and 2 above (Chapter Appendixes A and B). This should be true because both these groups of respondents—that is, those who are recent arrivals in the host country and those who have been in the host country for longer periods of time—should be in "up" periods as to attitudes and adaptation to the host cultures.

Furthermore, if the "U-curve" hypothesis is operating internationally in our data produced by this present investigation, crucial variables should display significant differences when we compare more recent with more long-term sojourners and those in between on the basis of Analyses 4 and 5 (Chapter Appendixes D and E). In other words, while the significant differences should not be evident when comparing those recent and long-term sojourners, significant differences should be evident when comparing those same recent and long-term sojourners with those in the middle. In addition, the significant differences in the latter analyses should evidence dissatisfaction or more negative attitudes on the part of those respondents in the middle, that is, those between the more recent and the more long-term sojourners, if the "U-curve" really exists.

For the sake of completeness, all sojourn categories are also presented on the basis of Analysis 3 above (Chapter Appendix C). The analysis was made to permit study of the direction of responses by duration of sojourn on all options presented to the students.

The "crucial variables" in the "U-curve" hypothesis should be the following:

1. The frequency of problems or difficulties reported by the respondents should vary with the duration of sojourn.

2. The reporting or not reporting of personal depression as a problem should vary with the duration.

3. The reporting of loneliness and homesickness in the respondents should vary with the duration.

4. Satisfaction or dissatisfaction with general regard to academic and to other (nonacademic) aspects of the sojourn experience should vary with the duration.

5. The ratings of the helpfulness of the teachers in general at the host institutions might also vary with the duration.

6. The reported opinion regarding the local people might vary with the duration.

The pattern of response regarding several other items, that is, the respondents' judgments with regard to the local people's knowledge of the home country, might also be expected to produce evidence of the international operation of the "U-curve." However, the items listed in Points 1 through 4 above are certainly the most crucial as to whether the "U-curve" hypothesis was or was not operating in the present international investigation. The case for the "U-curve" hypothesis would be even stronger if its operation is also evidenced in Points 5 and 6.

While the data underlying the analyses are presented in Chapter Appendixes A through E, the evidence for those variables that are here being considered crucial is presented in Table 9.1. In support of the "U-curve" hypothesis, no significant differences were located when more recent sojourners were compared with more long-term sojourners. This was true for all variables considered, with the single exception of general satisfaction versus dissatisfaction in regard to studies. Thus, one may initially suggest that the "U-curve" might be operating in the data, but an additional step is necessary.

Significant differences should then become evident when we analyze and compare those same recent and long-term sojourners with those in between. Furthermore, the significant differences should point to more dissatisfaction or negative attitudes on the part of the respondents in the middle, that is, those whose length of sojourn is in between the more recent and the more long-term sojourners.

In considering those with sojourns of 4 months or less, 5 to 24 months, and more than 2 years, we located significant differences on only two variables: (1) "many" compared with "some" compared with "few" problems or difficulties, and (2) general satisfaction compared with dissatisfaction in regard to studies. When we compared those with sojourns of 4 months or less, 5 to 8 months, and 9 to 12 months, significant differences were isolated only on a single variable: general satisfaction compared with dissatisfaction with regard to other aspects (nonacademic) of the sojourn experience. In other words, analyses of these three duration-of-sojourn divisions did not produce much evidence in support of a "U-curve" hypothesis, but one must still consider the direction of responses for the variables that have evidenced significant differences.

In terms of the direction of the significant findings, as was mentioned above, there were no significant differences between

TABLE 9.1

Significant Findings from Duration of Sojourn Analyses

	4 Months or Less vs. More than 2 Years	4 Months or Less vs. 9-12 Months	Under 1 Month, 1-4 Months, 5-8 Months, 9-12 Months, 13-18 Months, 19-24 Months, More than 2 Years	4 Months or Less vs. 5-24 Months vs. More than 2 Years	4 Months or Less vs. 5-8 Months vs. 9-12 Months
"Many" vs. "some" vs. "few" problems or difficulties					
Reporting vs. not reporting personal depression			*	*	
Loneliness					
Homesickness					
Satisfaction vs. dissatisfaction with general regard to studies	*	*	*	*	
Satisfaction vs. dissatisfaction with general regard to other aspects of the sojourn experience			*		
Rating helpfulness of teachers at the host institution			*		*
Reported opinion of local people			*		

*Significant at .01 level.
Source: Compiled by the authors.

123

more recent and more long-term sojourners with the single exception of one variable: general satisfaction compared with dissatisfaction in regard to studies. In this single case, the results indicated
that the more long-term sojourners were likely to report more general satisfaction with their studies than those more recent to the
host country, that is, those who had been in the host country for four
months or less. On all of the other variables where significant differences would be expected if the "U-curve" were operating, nothing
was found. Hence the set of analyses could not be considered sup-
portive of the "U-curve" hypothesis.

Satisfaction or dissatisfaction with academic aspects of the sojourn was judged to be a less sensitive indicator of the presence of
the "U-curve" than the other variables that displayed no significant
differences. That is to say, the "U-curve" hypothesis, being more
concerned with adjustment patterns and attitudes, should share a
close relationship to the variables inherent in the problems reported—
personal depression, loneliness, homesickness, satisfaction or dissatisfaction with nonacademic aspects of the sojourn—but it did not.

With regard to the next set of analyses, significant differences
in the direction that would exhibit a "U" pattern should be evident in
the data produced by the variables not found to be significant in the
above paragraph. Significant differences appeared in three variables.
Those sojourners who had been in the host country for the longest
period of time, that is, more than 2 years, were the most likely to
be in the group indicating "few problems" and were also the most
likely to show a higher degree of satisfaction with their studies.
However, a "U" pattern within the responses with regard to sojourn
durations of 4 months or less, 5 to 24 months, and more than 2
years, was simply not present. At most, one could only point to a
very weak "J" pattern. Furthermore, the other significant difference indicated that the more long-term sojourners (in this case,
those who had been in the host country from 9 to 12 months) were
the most likely to indicate the least general satisfaction with nonacademic aspects of their sojourn. No "U" pattern was evident in
these data either, however. If anything, the pattern was a slightly
upside down "U," indicating that sojourners in the middle duration
group (in this case, those who had been in the host country from 5
to 8 months) were more likely to be generally satisfied with regard
to the nonacademic aspects of their experience than were either the
more recent or more long-term sojourners.

A great deal more could be discussed here, but it is more important to note that there were no significant differences (and consequently no patterns in any way resembling a "U-curve") for any of
the other variables that were previously mentioned as crucial. That
is to say, there were no significant differences based on duration of

sojourn in regard to: (1) personal depression, (2) loneliness, (3) homesickness, (4) helpfulness of teachers at the host institution, or (5) opinion regarding the local people.

Furthermore, as a result of further analyses on the basis of all of the duration-of-sojourn options available (that is, under 1 month, 1-4 months, 5-8 months, 9-12 months, 13-18 months, 19-24 months, and more than 2 years), additional significant differences were located (Table 9.1), but in none of the variables where such significant differences were found was a "U" pattern in evidence.

It must, therefore, be concluded that in terms of the hard data analyses performed for the present international investigation, almost no support was found for the "U-curve" hypothesis. Methodological criteria preclude any conclusion that the hypothesis is completely invalid, but it is equally certain that the present data do not encourage any assumption of its validity.

INTERNATIONAL LONGITUDINAL INTERVIEW DATA

The interviews with foreign students in a number of countries were specifically conducted in part because of our interest in the "U-curve" hypothesis. In the first place, one important implication of the "U-curve," assuming that it does exist, is that the interviews of foreign students designed to determine their reactions to their sojourns abroad may be greatly influenced by the precise point on the curve at which the student happens to be when being questioned. This represents a research hazard that is very difficult to control, since the curve will vary in particular shape from one individual and one situation to another, and from intensity to nonexistence. The rise in the curve with regard to satisfaction may be steep or shallow or may occur as a kind of "sleeper effect" when the student returns home.

This led us to conduct three interviews with these students, one as near as possible to their time of arrival; the second about midway during their academic year; the third toward the end of that year. We felt that this more clinical approach to each individual student would add essential information which would go beyond that obtainable at a single point in the sojourn.

Secondly, we thought that three interviews with the same student should give us direct evidence as to whether or not the "U-curve" is a truly characteristic phenomenon. If it is, we should expect to find a marked tendency for euphoria and excitement to appear during the first interview, signs of anxiety or depression during the second, and a return to a degree of satisfaction during the third. We admit that there may be some oversimplification in this approach, in part because it was limited to one academic year, and in part also as a result of the fact that the phases of the curve, particularly the depression and the recovery from it, would not necessarily occur at the same period of time in the case of all students. We feel on safe ground, however, in our answers to the following questions. Does the sojourn always, or usually, begin with euphoria? Is there always, or usually, a period of depression? Does the sojourn always, or usually, end with a feeling of satisfaction as problems are solved and difficulties overcome? Our data from these interviews lead us to give a definitely negative answer to the first question; to express doubt with regard to the second; and on the whole to answer the third in the affirmative. For the "U-curve" as a whole, we would conclude that it does occur, but only in a small minority of cases.

In an earlier study, conducted by one of the authors with J. Ben Brika[6] and dealing with students from the Third World enrolled at universities in Paris, Vienna, The Hague, and Ljubljana, the following conclusions emerged.

Approximately 650 students were interviewed; they hailed from Africa, Asia, Latin America, North Africa, and the Middle East. We were interested in discovering the factors contributing to varying degrees of satisfaction with the foreign sojourn, and to test some of the hypotheses which had previously been raised in the (predominantly American) literature.

The results of that study showed that a very substantial proportion of the foreign students reported that they had been worried and anxious about going abroad. This was the case with more than half of those who were in Austria, and with 82 percent of those in France. These figures were not only considerably higher than we had anticipated, but also raised in our minds certain questions regarding the kinds of persons who look forward to a foreign sojourn, and those who are disturbed by the prospect. They also made us wonder about the "U-curve." If anxiety begins at home, so to speak, what happens to the alleged initial period of euphoria and good adjustment which is supposed to be characteristic of the first experience abroad?

As part of this present investigation, we conducted interviews in France with 28 foreign students during the 1976–77 academic year, 22 in Paris, and 6 in Nice. They were interviewed on three separate occasions: first, at the end of October or the beginning of November 1976; second in January, and third and last between April 25 and May 25, 1977. A majority of these students (15) felt lost, lonely, and depressed at the beginning of their sojourns. In their case, there was no evidence of an initial euphoria.

Most of the students interviewed in France ended their year with expressions of satisfaction, although there were a few (7) exceptions. A small minority (3) started out happy and remained so during their whole sojourn. Only 2 cases showed the pattern expected on the basis of the "U-curve" hypothesis.

We realize that the number of cases we interviewed in France is too small to make the above figures significant, but they seem to us to be adequate as indicating that the typical "U-curve" appears relatively rarely. Depression does occur with some frequency, but may manifest itself much earlier in the experience than would be predicted on the basis of the "U-curve." We feel justified in arguing that these interviews demonstrate that the "U-curve" is the exception rather than the rule.

The interviews in other countries point in the same direction. Out of 19 interviews in Brazil, for the most part with students from other countries in Latin America, 12 cases reported depression on the occasion of the first interview. One student started out happy and optimistic, and became increasingly depressed and worried as time went on: three were happy at the beginning of their sojourn and remained so throughout; one was unhappy at the first and continued to be depressed all the way. The majority (13) were satisfied and relatively happy by the end of the academic year. There was no single case that followed the exact pattern predicted on the basis of the "U-curve."

Out of 21 foreign students interviewed in the United States, a majority (13) showed anxiety and depression at the first interview, although in a number of instances not too serious in character, and usually showed improvement as the year went on. Six cases reported no real depression at any time, and only one (a Belgian studying at a private Midwestern university) followed the phases of the "U-curve" with almost textbook accuracy.

Two additional issues regarding the "U-curve" seem to us to require comment. The first is a consequence of the finding that depression does occur with some frequency, although to different degrees and at different times during the academic year. Knowledge of this fact may itself have a certain therapeutic value. Whatever it is in human history that gave rise to the saying that "misery loves company," it appears certain that depression is more easily coped with when it is known that many others have gone through the same experience.

In the second place, when depression is truly serious or lasts too long, the student may require professional help. This leads to the important issue as to whether problems related to mental illness occur more frequently among foreign than among native students, and consequently as to what can be done to help them. The general impression appears to be that cases of psychological maladjustment occur more frequently among foreign than among native students, although many cases may never really "come to light" and thus may not appear in available statistics. This whole issue is the subject of a somewhat recent review by Alexander et al.[7] which touches on many of the issues already considered in this chapter, such as the feeling of isolation and loneliness. The authors, on the basis of their own investigation of Asian and African students in the United States, suggest that such feelings are much more widespread than is usually assumed. They write: ". . . our research has shown that the vast majority of non-Western or Third World students . . . feel vulnerable and at risk during much of their time in the United States."[8] They go on to speak of the "painful social vulnerability" of the students, their lack of contact with Americans, and the fact that they are "fearful and pessimistic" about the possibility of establishing better social contact.

The general conclusions of the research are as follows:

1. Foreign students are a high risk group, under considerable stress.

2. This stress is more likely to be experienced in the form of physical complaints than psychological complaints.

3. The foreign student is more likely to seek medical than psychological help, with the latter sought only after all other resources have been exhausted.

4. There is considerable commonality to foreign students' psychosomatic and emotional problems.[9]

The authors make another important point, namely, that as clinicians they are convinced that when foreign students ask for help with emotional problems, they are in greater need of help than their American counterparts. This is because foreign students are more reluctant to ask for professional help, since such resources are usually not easily available in the home country, and because the admission of such a need would constitute a loss of status. This would imply that statistics comparing the proportion of appeals for help would underestimate the frequency of such needs in the case of foreign students.

We believe that this estimate of the frequency of mental illness among foreign students has been exaggerated, but obviously when it does occur, it may represent a very serious problem, and steps must be taken to deal with it. This raises the whole issue of "counseling across cultures," which is the title of an important recent publication edited by Pedersen et al.[10] The authors point out that cultural sensitivity on the part of the counselor has recently been considered to be an ethical imperative. In his chapter on the field of intercultural counseling, Pedersen remarks that:

The American Psychological Association sponsored a
conference on patterns and levels of professional
training at Vail, Colorado, in July 1963. One of the
recommendations of that conference was that the counseling of persons of culturally diverse backgrounds by
persons who are not trained or competent to work with
such groups should be regarded as unethical. . . . It
is apparent that cultural sensitivity and awareness will
play an increasingly important role in the training of
counselors. [11]

Pedersen believes that the trained counselor is not usually prepared
to deal with members of groups whose values, attitudes, and general
life styles differ from the counselor's own.

In another chapter in the same volume, "Racial and Ethnic
Barriers in Counseling," Vontress gives a number of specific examples of the difficulties that may arise. Clients from some cultures show less openness and are unable to speak freely of their own
troubles to a comparative stranger; this is true of American Indians,
who usually communicate so little as to render the counseling process
largely ineffective. Japanese-Americans may hesitate to express
their feelings in the presence of individuals of higher status. In a
later chapter, Sundberg refers to the great difference between students from India and Americans "in regard to decision-making—a
very important aspect of counseling young people."[12] A number of
years ago, Gardner Murphy reported[13] that in India a greater change
in attitudes occurred when students were addressed by an authority
figure than when they arrived at a group decision. This finding has
since been confirmed by subsequent research.[14] Sundberg points out
that there are other Indian cultural factors that affect the process of
counseling interaction. The concept of privacy and openness is not
the same as in the United States; certain family matters are not mentioned to outsiders such as counselors; non-directive counseling may
be interpreted as meaning rejection or lack of interest in the Indian
client. Sundberg adds that all of these factors, together with differences in customs, make the transfer of counseling to Indians a serious
problem. After raising the question as to whether perhaps too much
stress may have been placed on cultural factors, he writes: "Most
of us in counseling are left between the two dangers of being overly
concerned with cultural differences and being not concerned
enough. . . ."[15]

As far as practical implications are concerned, it has already
been indicated that foreign students might be helped through their depressive stage (when that does occur) if they learn that their experience is by no means exceptional in this regard. The counselor,

on the other hand, should be aware of the tremendous variations that the "U-curve" undergoes from individual to individual, for example, in the length of time during which each stage lasts, the intensity with which it is experienced, and even the presence or absence of one or another of the stages. The "U-curve" is not inevitable as a description of the course of the total sojourn, and it is just as much of a mistake to take it too seriously as to ignore the fact that depression does occur with some frequency, and that it may create very real problems for some of the students concerned. We should add, however, that cases of acute depression requiring professional treatment were rare as far as our data are concerned.

One final point. We have spoken so far in this chapter of depression in the case of students abroad. The question arises as to whether it occurs also in the case of teachers or professors, Fulbright scholars, and others at a relatively mature stage in their development. There is one problem which our research has identified as occurring with some frequency among professors at a foreign university, and which may have very unfavorable consequences for the sojourn as a whole. Too often the foreign professor on arrival receives inadequate information as to what is expected, and no clear indication of the "slot" into which he should try to fit. Therefore, a considerable portion of the sojourn must be spent in creating a satisfying role. Sometimes, the foreign professor may fail in this attempt and spend an unhappy year; sometimes that professor may become so disturbed by the experience as to leave before the year is over. We can testify from our own observations that these reactions do occur, although we are convinced that such cases are in the minority. There are unfortunately very few investigations of these subjective aspects of the foreign experience at the professorial level.

Thus, in conclusion, while we have not found data in support of the "U-curve" hypothesis, we have argued that depressive reactions may occur regularly throughout the world and that this is an area where preplanning as well as professional awareness and readiness to provide assistance is imperative.

NOTES

1. Sverre Lysgaard, "Adjustment in a Foreign Society: Norwegian Fulbright Grantees Visiting the United States," International Social Science Bulletin 7 (1955): 45-51, and A Study of Intercultural Contact: Norwegian Fulbright Grantees Visiting the United States (Oslo: Institute for Social Research, 1954).

2. See S. Lundstedt, "An Introduction to Some Evolving Problems in Cross-Cultural Research," Journal of Social Issues 19 (July 1963): 1-9, and John T. Gullahorn and Jeanne E. Gullahorn, "An Extension of the U-Curve Hypothesis," Journal of Social Issues 19 (July 1963): 33-47.

3. Richard T. Morris, The Two-Way Mirror: National Status in Foreign Student Adjustment (Minneapolis: University of Minnesota Press, 1960), p. 105 et passim.

4. George V. Coelho, Changing Images of America: A Study of Indian Students' Perceptions (Glencoe, Ill.: Free Press, 1958).

5. W. Frank Hull IV, Foreign Students in the United States of America: Coping Behavior within the Educational Environment (New York: Praeger, 1978), Chapter 10, pp. 143-44.

6. Otto Klineberg and J. Ben Brika, Etudiants du Tiers-Monde en Europe (Paris: Mouton, 1972).

7. A. A. Alexander et al., "Psychotherapy and the Foreign Student," in Paul Pedersen et al., Counseling across Cultures (Honolulu: University of Hawaii Press, 1976).

8. Ibid., p. 83.

9. Ibid., pp. 87, 88.

10. Paul Pedersen et al., Counseling across Cultures (Honolulu: University of Hawaii Press, 1976).

11. Ibid., pp. 35, 36.

12. Ibid., p. 164.

13. Gardner Murphy, In the Minds of Men (New York: Basic Books, 1953).

14. See Pedersen et al., op. cit.

15. Ibid., p. 141.

CHAPTER APPENDIXES

Appendix A: Cross Tabulations: The Variable
of Duration of Sojourn

Item: Sojourns of 4 months or less vs. more than 2 years

	Chi Square	Degrees of Freedom
"Traveled" vs. "nontraveled" respondents	0.0001	1
"Lots of contact" vs. "medium" vs. "little contact"	12.763	2*
Geographic "origin" of respondents	89.627	12*
Nationality of others "when in the company of others"	3.822	3
Nationality of "best friend" in the host country	4.005	3
Person with whom lodging is shared	45.833	5*
"Many" vs. "some" vs. "few" problems or difficulties	3.914	2
Reporting vs. not reporting personal depression	0.0001	1
Reporting vs. not reporting personal discrimination	19.169	1*
Reported opinion of the local people (pre-arrival)	1.819	2
Reported opinion of the local people (at point of research)	0.311	2
Loneliness	6.372	4
Homesickness	8.319	4
Rating of teaching quality at the host institution	11.563	5
Rating helpfulness of teachers at the host institution	5.052	5
"High" vs. "medium" vs. "low" impact as a result of the experience of living in the host country	39.496	2*
Satisfaction vs. dissatisfaction with general regard to studies	36.594	4*
Satisfaction vs. dissatisfaction with general regard to other aspects of the sojourn experience	5.991	4
Local people's knowledge of home country	1.292	1
Local people's attitude toward home country	17.407	2*

*Significant at the .01 level.

N.B. The particulars of the cross tabulations are explained in Chapter 11.

Appendix B: Cross Tabulations: The Variable
of Duration of Sojourn

Item: Sojourns of 4 months or less vs. 9 to 12 months

	Chi Square	Degrees of Freedom
"Traveled" vs. "nontraveled" respondents	1.781	1
"Lots of contact" vs. "medium" vs. "little contact"	2.241	2
Geographic "origin" of respondents	46.011	12*
Nationality of others "when in the company of others"	8.005	3
Nationality of "best friend" in the host country	6.585	3
Person with whom lodging is shared	34.682	5*
"Many" vs. "some" vs. "few" problems or difficulties	4.010	2
Reporting vs. not reporting personal depression	1.657	1
Reporting vs. not reporting personal discrimination	0.061	1
Reported opinion of the local people (pre-arrival)	0.856	2
Reported opinion of the local people (at point of research)	1.563	2
Loneliness	9.766	4
Homesickness	4.008	4
Rating of teaching quality at the host institution	6.314	5
Rating helpfulness of teachers at the host institution	13.778	5
"High" vs. "medium" vs. "low" impact as a result of the experience of living in the host country	0.696	2
Satisfaction vs. dissatisfaction with general regard to studies	13.122	4*
Satisfaction vs. dissatisfaction with general regard to other aspects of the sojourn experience	4.022	4
Local people's knowledge of home country	6.011	2
Local people's attitude toward home country	4.630	2

*Significant at the .01 level.
N.B. The particulars of the cross tabulations are explained in Chapter 11.

Appendix C: Cross Tabulations: The Variable
of Duration of Sojourn

Item: Sojourns of under 1 month, 1 to 4 months, 5 to 8 months, 9 to
12 months, 13 to 18 months, 19 to 24 months, more than 2 years

	Chi Square	Degrees of Freedom
"Traveled" vs. "nontraveled" respondents	14.379	6
"Lots of contact" vs. "medium" vs. "little contact"	29.306	12*
Geographic "origin" of respondents	314.664	72*
Nationality of others "when in the company of others"	32.174	18
Nationality of "best friend" in the host country	30.912	18
Person with whom lodging is shared	119.852	30*
"Many" vs. "some" vs. "few" problems or difficulties	29.607	12*
Reporting vs. not reporting personal depression	6.143	6
Reporting vs. not reporting personal discrimination	85.336	6*
Reported opinion of the local people (pre-arrival)	21.280	12
Reported opinion of the local people (at point of research)	36.823	12*
Loneliness	38.486	24
Homesickness	34.761	24
Rating of teaching quality at the host institution	47.923	30
Rating helpfulness of teachers at the host institution	50.818	30*
"High" vs. "medium" vs. "low" impact as a result of the experience of living in the host country	185.617	12*
Satisfaction vs. dissatisfaction with general regard to studies	60.816	24*
Satisfaction vs. dissatisfaction with general regard to other aspects of the sojourn experience	44.526	24*
Local people's knowledge of home country	71.302	12*
Local people's attitude toward home country	45.391	12*

*Significant at the .01 level.
N.B. The particulars of the cross tabulations are explained in
Chapter 11.

Appendix D: Cross Tabulations: The Variable
of Duration of Sojourn

Item: Sojourns of 4 months or less vs. 5 to 24 months vs. more
than 2 years

	Chi Square	Degrees of Freedom
"Traveled" vs. "nontraveled" respondents	4.011	2
"Lots of contact" vs. "medium" vs. "little contact"	15.810	4*
Geographic "origin" of respondents	165.117	24*
Nationality of others "when in the company of others"	8.438	6
Nationality of "best friend" in the host country	8.322	6
Person with whom lodging is shared	67.112	10*
"Many" vs. "some" vs. "few" problems or difficulties	19.244	4*
Reporting vs. not reporting personal depression	0.490	2
Reporting vs. not reporting personal discrimination	72.348	2*
Reported opinion of the local people (pre-arrival)	2.602	4
Reported opinion of the local people (at point of research)	6.130	4
Loneliness	13.779	8
Homesickness	12.462	8
Rating of teaching quality at the host institution	19.650	10
Rating helpfulness of teachers at the host institution	17.311	10
"High" vs. "medium" vs. "low" impact as a result of the experience of living in the host country	136.181	4*
Satisfaction vs. dissatisfaction with general regard to studies	39.492	8*
Satisfaction vs. dissatisfaction with general regard to other aspects of the sojourn experience	12.454	8
Local people's knowledge of home country	39.661	4*
Local people's attitude toward home country	31.227	4*

*Significant at the .01 level.
N.B. The particulars of the cross tabulations are explained in
Chapter 11.

Appendix E: Cross Tabulations: The Variable
of Duration of Sojourn

Item: Sojourns of 4 months or less vs. 5 to 8 months vs. 9 to 12
months

	Chi Square	Degrees of Freedom
"Traveled" vs. "nontraveled" respondents	2.316	2
"Lots of contact" vs. "medium" vs. "little contact"	12.524	4
Geographic "origin" of respondents	62.084	24*
Nationality of others "when in the company of others"	16.746	6
Nationality of "best friend" in the host country	9.900	6
Person with whom lodging is shared	45.687	10*
"Many" vs. "some" vs. "few" problems or difficulties	6.816	4
Reporting vs. not reporting personal depression	3.932	2
Reporting vs. not reporting personal discrimination	0.463	2
Reported opinion of the local people (pre-arrival)	1.774	4
Reported opinion of the local people (at point of research)	3.812	4
Loneliness	14.896	8
Homesickness	9.271	8
Rating of teaching quality at the host institution	19.792	10
Rating helpfulness of teachers at the host institution	19.484	10
"High" vs. "medium" vs. "low" impact as a result of the experience of living in the host country	4.196	4
Satisfaction vs. dissatisfaction with general regard to studies	19.667	8
Satisfaction vs. dissatisfaction with general regard to other aspects of the sojourn experience	23.386	8*
Local people's knowledge of home country	6.994	4
Local people's attitude toward home country	11.421	4

*Significant at the .01 level.

N.B. The particulars of the cross tabulations are explained in
Chapter 11.

10

NATIONAL PROFILES

In this chapter we present a description in summary form of the principal characteristics and the experience of foreign students in each of the 11 countries included in our investigation. Since the discussion in the preceding chapters and the tables that have been analyzed have to a considerable extent been based on the actual percentages of the responses obtained in answer to the questions posed in this investigation, we shall limit ourselves in this chapter to a summary profile. This will consist of a more qualitative account of where the foreign students in each specific country stand with regard to the total number of respondents and will indicate in both absolute and relative terms the frequency of both the difficulties and the satisfactions that they experienced during their sojourn.

(1) Brazil. Foreign students in Brazil (149 respondents) came mainly from other Latin American countries. The sample was almost three-fourths male and most likely to be studying the life-biological sciences, with engineering-physical sciences in second place. In the international sample as a whole the latter subject was most popular, with the behavioral sciences in second place.

About half of the respondents felt that they had received at least reasonable information regarding study in Brazil before leaving home. They were in second place in terms of their academic as well as their general and social satisfaction, and well above the average as far as their positive feelings about their studies and their social experiences were concerned. In all of these respects, satisfaction was high in absolute as well as relative terms.

On the other hand, they complained the most frequently of insufficient previous training, the difficulty of the courses, and problems with examinations, and very frequently also of lack of personal

counseling. They were above average in the frequency of their difficulties regarding food, climate, finances, problems concerning
the "credits" received for previous academic work, lack of a private
place to study, and adequate contact with local fellow students. They
also complained with more than average frequency of difficulty with
the local language, dealings with the university administration, and
lack of adequate information regarding progress in their studies.
They were, however, less likely than the average to express concern about too little contact with local people, about lack of direction in their studies, and rarely reported difficulties in relations
with the opposite sex. As for housing, they were in second place in
terms of frequency of complaints regarding the difficulty of finding
adequate housing, and as to the problem of local transport. They
were also well above average in references to the excessive expense
involved and the lack of personal privacy, but they referred relatively infrequently to problems regarding comfort and cleanliness.
Their most troublesome problems related to finances and to insufficient previous training.

As far as relationg with the teaching staff were concerned,
they were in second place in their appreciation of the teaching quality and the accessibility of teachers, and well above average in their
judgment of the intellectual stimulation and the personal helpfulness
that teachers supplied.

With regard to the important area of contact with others, these
students were in second place as far as frequency of contact with
local students was concerned, and first in terms of the likelihood
that their best friend would be a local student. They were also the
most frequent to report opportunities for social contact with, and invitations to visit, local families, and they were well above average
in having meals with the local population, and in finding that their
contacts with them were as frequent as they could have wished.

In the realm of international relations, they were the most frequent to assert that the local population had no reasonable knowledge
about their (the foreign students') country of origin, but were above
average in judging their attitude to be favorable or very favorable.
These students started out (in second place) with a good early opinion
of the local population, and maintained this position at the time of
this investigation. They were the least likely of all the 11 country
samples to report that either they themselves or their friends and
relatives had suffered discrimination during the sojourn in Brazil.
They were, however, the most frequent to report that they had felt
depressed during the stay abroad (although, as reported above, this
depression usually disappeared with time, and was not regarded as
too serious). About one-sixth of the foreign students would like to
remain in Brazil.

As for the impact of the foreign sojourn, these students were above average in reporting positive changes in their intellectual development, their self-confidence, and their general personal development. They were about average as to changes in feelings of independence, and, like all the other country samples, found that they had altered very little with regard to their political opinions or religious attitudes. They were well above average in reporting either that the sojourn had made them more positive about their own country or had had no effect. They were the least likely to report that their foreign sojourn had made them more negative in this respect.

(2) Canada. In Canada, foreign students (N = 620) came from a large variety of countries, with the largest single groups from the United States, Hong Kong, the United Kingdom, and France. Approximately seven out of ten were male, and more than half were in engineering-physical sciences or in life-biological sciences. A substantial majority felt at least reasonably well informed about Canada before arrival. They were about average (and favorable) in their judgment of the overall academic experience as well as their general and social experience at the university. As for difficulties, they were in third place regarding the frequency of depression and a feeling of insufficient previous training; they were in second place with regard to lack of contact with local people, and slightly above average in the frequency of a similar complaint with regard to local students. They had little difficulty in adjusting to local food, were a little below the average in financial worries, and for the other problems and difficulties listed were close to or below the average in frequency. As for housing, they were in third place in complaints regarding excessive expense, but otherwise they were near or below the average. In general, the two most troublesome problems related to finances and climate.

The judgments regarding the teaching staff were in general definitely favorable; they were in second place regarding the accessibility of the majority of teachers (but equal to Brazil, Kenya, and the United Kingdom in this respect), and well above average with regard to teaching quality, helpfulness, and intellectual stimulation.

As far as relations with others are concerned, foreign students in Canada were among the least likely (after Hong Kong and France) to report frequent contacts with local students, to have a local student as a roommate (after Iran and France), or as a best friend. They were well below average in terms of opportunities for social contact with local families, in invitations to visit in local homes, or to have meals or other social contacts with the local population. This seems to be a fairly general characteristic of the sojourn in Canada, although not quite so pronounced as in the case of certain other countries.

These students were about average in judging that the local population knew relatively little about their (the foreign students') country of origin, and somewhat below average in judging that the opinion was a favorable one. They had a favorable opinion (at about the average level for the 11 countries) of Canada on arrival, and it remained favorable. A relatively large proportion (not far from 50 percent) reported that they had friends or relatives who had suffered discrimination (second in frequency among the 11 countries), dropping to about one in three who reported a similar experience of their own (close to the average in this respect). Slightly more than one-sixth of them, however, would like to stay on in Canada if possible (the second highest proportion, exceeded only by Hong Kong with one-fourth).

With regard to the impact of the sojourn as perceived by the students in Canada, the frequency was well above the average in personal and intellectual development, in feelings of self-confidence and of independence, and also in changes in political opinions. The majority judged that the sojourn had had no effect on their view of their own country; about one-third became more positive, and about one in eight more negative.

(3) France. The foreign students in France (96 respondents) came from a large variety of countries, with a substantial proportion from former French colonies in Africa and Southeast Asia. About seven out of ten were male, and they were predominantly studying arts-humanities and the engineering-physical sciences. Slightly over half stated that they had obtained adequate information before leaving their home countries, but close to 50 percent found that even in France they were unable to obtain information which they regarded as satisfactory. Six out of ten were either satisfied or very satisfied with their academic experience, and about one-half were satisfied with their overall general and social experience at the university; in both cases this was below the average for the 11 countries.

Students in France led all the rest in complaints about absence of adequate contact with local fellow students and the local population in general, and also about a lack of framework and direction in their academic program. They were also above average in frequency with regard to financial problems, personal depression, and difficulties in adjusting to climate, and in connection with relations with the opposite sex. They were at or near the average in most of the other problems we have been considering, and had less difficulty than the average student with academic courses or with adjusting to the local food. As for housing, they complained more than any others regarding the expense involved. In general, their most troublesome difficulties related to finances and relations with the opposite sex.

With regard to the teaching staff, a complaint raised more often in France than anywhere else referred to their inaccessibility in the majority of cases. Teachers were also ranked somewhat below the average for their helpfulness, the intellectual stimulation they provided, and their teaching quality, but it was their inaccessibility that produced by far the most striking results.

In the area of contact with others, foreign students in France reported the least frequently that they had made good friends since their arrival, but there were still seven out of ten who answered in the affirmative. Their roommate was very rarely a local student, and they were least likely to report that their best friend was a local student. They reported few opportunities for social contact with the local population, for visits to local families, or having meals with local people in the neighborhood (although this last item occurred even more rarely in Japan and Iran).

Students in France were far above the average in finding that the local population had an inadequate knowledge of their (the foreign students') country, but were exceeded in this respect by those in Brazil and the United States; they were about average in their feeling that the local attitude toward their countries was either favorable or very favorable. Their own judgment of the French was relatively favorable at the outset of the sojourn, and about average for the 11 countries; it fell considerably by the time they were questioned, ending up below all others although remaining somewhat favorable. As for discrimination, slightly more than half stated that they had no friends or relatives who had had that experience in France, and six out of ten had no such experience of their own to report. This shows a level of discrimination above the average, but this difference is small. When asked about their preference for the future, about one foreign student in seven would like to stay in France; this is above the average. (We have referred above to the paradox of liking the French less, but France more, as a consequence of the sojourn.)

The general judgment regarding the impact of a stay at a French university is seen as about average for personal and intellectual development; above average for political opinions, and below for feelings of self-confidence and independence. These students also occupy an average position in terms of becoming more positive about their own country, but slightly above for the development of more negative attitudes (explained by a relatively high percentage reporting no effect).

(4) The Federal Republic of Germany. There were 42 respondents in West Germany, with slightly more male than female students. They came mainly from Europe, but with the largest single group from the United States. A very large proportion (about two-thirds)

studied arts-humanities. Three out of four reported having received adequate or fair information before departure; one-third found that even after arrival there was difficulty in obtaining information which they considered adequate.

About three out of four were satisfied with their overall academic experience as well as with their general and social experience; in both of these respects they were well above the average, and high also in absolute terms. Problems and difficulties which received the most frequent mention included the question of equivalence or proper placement level upon arrival (in which they were in second place, but fairly low in absolute terms, affecting about one student in five) and insufficient previous training and difficulty in adjusting to local food, in which the frequency was somewhat above average. On the other hand they were below average in frequency of references to the lack of personal counseling, problems with examinations, or difficulty with the local language; relatively very low (in tenth place) with regard to finances, personal depression, lack of information regarding progress in studies, and difficulties with the university administration. They complained the least frequently of all the country samples about relations with the opposite sex, lack of contact with local students or other local people, and (together with students in Hong Kong) about difficulties with courses. They ranked as their most troublesome problems the question of placement level on arrival, and (strangely enough) lack of contact with local people. As regards housing, they were the least troubled by finances, and to a relatively slight degree by other factors which students elsewhere frequently found annoying.

With regard to the teaching staff, they were about average in their judgment of the teaching quality in general, the intellectual stimulation provided, and the accessibility of the majority of teachers; they were relatively less positive (in tenth place) as to the helpfulness of teachers.

They reported more commonly than any other samples that their most frequent contacts were with local students, and were second (exceeded only in Brazil) in the frequency with which they stated that their best friend was a local student. They were also far above the average in their opportunities for social contact with local families, in visits to their homes, in positive relations, and the sharing of meals with people in the neighborhood.

In the area of international relations, they were the most frequent (together with foreign students in Kenya) to feel that the local population had an adequate knowledge of their (the foreign students') country, and in second place in feeling that the local attitude toward these countries was either favorable or very favorable. They started out with a relatively positive judgment of West Germany

before arrival, which decreased slightly by the time of the interview but remained favorable. They were less likely than students
in other countries (except for Brazil) to report that they had friends
or relatives who had experienced discrimination, or that they themselves had had such an experience. On the other hand, they were
about average in expressing a desire to remain in West Germany
rather than return home.

In relation to the perceived impact of the sojourn, foreign students in West Germany were below average in reporting changes in
personal and intellectual development, and in feelings of self-
confidence and independence. They were, on the other hand, the
most likely of all, in relative terms, to report that their political
opinions had changed. They were also high (in second place) in finding that they had become more positive about their own country.

It should be pointed out that the sample in West Germany is
small, and it is restricted to one relatively small university in a
relatively small town. The results should therefore be considered
as hypotheses rather than as a definitive account of foreign students
in general in that country.

(5) Hong Kong. The foreign student sample (42 respondents) included North Americans as the largest single group, and was almost
equally divided, as was the case in West Germany, between men and
women. They were mainly (more than in any other country) in the
behavioral-social sciences and secondly in the arts-humanities.

Exactly 50 percent felt that before arrival they had received
adequate or fair information regarding their foreign sojourn, but
one in four complained that since arriving there had been difficulty
in obtaining all the information needed. They were in last place as
far as satisfaction with their academic experience was concerned,
and well below average with regard to their general and social experience (but as we noted above, in all countries more than half the
respondents were either satisfied or very satisfied). With regard
to problems and difficulties, they were the least likely among all
samples to complain about finances, lack of personal counseling,
problems with examinations, the difficulty of the courses, or of insufficient previous training; they were well below average in the frequency of complaints regarding lack of framework or direction in
their studies, problems of equivalence or proper placement, and
lack of contact with local students or the general population, and
they had relatively little difficulty in adjusting to local food. They
did have problems, however, with the local climate and considerable difficulty with regard to language. As for housing, they were
the least likely to mention lack of general comfort. In spite of the
low frequency with which they complained about finances, they still
ranked that as their most troublesome problem.

With regard to teachers, the foreign students in Hong Kong were the least enthusiastic about the teaching quality in general and not at all positive about the intellectual stimulation provided; they were somewhat above average in ratings of their teachers' helpfulness, however, and below average with regard to their accessibility.

In the social area, these students were the most frequent to report having a local student as a roommate, but below the average in reporting that their best friend was a local student. A very large proportion (nine out of ten) stated, however, that they had made good friends since their arrival. They were below average in opportunities for contact with the local population, in visiting local families, or having meals together with local people.

As for international relations, they were above average in judging that the people in Hong Kong had a reasonably accurate knowledge of their (the foreign students') home countries, and also in feeling that the attitude toward their countries was favorable or very favorable. Their own opinion of the Hong Kong people was relatively positive on arrival, and became a little less so by the time of this investigation. About one in four (above average for the 11 samples) reported that friends or relatives had experienced discrimination, and more than one-third (the second highest) stated that they themselves had had such an experience. This is a reversal of the more usual finding in this investigation that there is more discrimination against "others" than against oneself. These students were in first place (one in four) to express a preference for remaining in the area of their sojourn if they had the choice. They were close to the average in judging that they had become more positive about their own country.

As to the impact of the sojourn abroad, they were about average in reporting a positive change in personal development, but well below with regard to feelings of independence and intellectual development, and least likely to indicate a gain in self-confidence.

Once again, the small sample must lead to caution in generalizations as to foreign students in Hong Kong. It is of course true that Hong Kong is not a nation or a country in the same political sense as the others, but we felt that it is different enough in terms of its ethnic and geographical characteristics to warrant inclusion in this investigation.

(6) India. The sample consisted of 56 foreign students, four out of five male, coming mainly from other Asian and South Asian countries as well as from Mauritius. They were mainly studying arts-humanities, with scattered representation in other areas.

They were about average in reporting that the information received before leaving was reasonably satisfactory, and that what they had obtained after arrival was adequate. They were the least likely to state that they were very satisfied with their overall academic experience, but only slightly below average if the percentages for "satisfied" and "very satisfied" are combined. With regard to the overall general and social experience, they were somewhat below the average in expressing satisfaction.

The foreign students in India expressed a wide variety of complaints. They were the most likely of all to mention lack of information regarding progress in studies, difficulties in dealing with the university administration, and (by far) adjustment to the local food and the climate. They also led (but the absolute proportion was still small) in mentioning problems relating to religion. They were in second place in the frequency of depression, in financial problems, complaints about relations with the opposite sex, lack of framework and direction in academic programs, problems with examinations, and insufficient previous training. They were also well above average in referring to the lack of personal counseling and difficulty with the local language, as well as lack of contact with the local population, but less frequently than the average with regard to contact with local students. As for lodgings they were the most frequent (by far) to complain of lack of cleanliness, and also of general comfort, difficulties with transportation, and distance from shopping areas. They complained considerably more than the average regarding the distance between their lodgings and the university, but less frequently than the average of the excessive expense involved. Their most troublesome problem was in adjusting to local food.

As far as their teachers were concerned, these students were at or close to the average in judgments of the teaching quality in general, the intellectual stimulation provided, the helpfulness and accessibility of the majority of teachers.

These students were also at or close to the average in reporting that their contacts were mainly with local students, that their roommate and also their best friend in the country was a local student, and above average (nine out of ten) in reporting that they had made good friends since their arrival. They were above average in terms of positive contacts with their neighbors and having meals with them, but below average in having social relations with local families or being invited into their homes.

They were a little below the average in judging that the local people had a reasonably accurate knowledge of their (the foreign students') countries, but they were the most frequent of all the samples in believing that the local people had a favorable or very favorable attitude toward those countries. Their own feelings about the Indians before arrival were less positive than the average of the 11 countries, but were favorable in general, and became a little less so by the time they were questioned. They were close to the average in reporting that friends or relatives had suffered discrimination or that they themselves had had that experience; the proportion remained the same (about three out of ten). A relatively small proportion (only in Kenya was there a lower percentage) expressed a preference for staying on in India. About one-third (the third lowest out of 11) said they had become more positive about their own country as a consequence of their foreign sojourn.

As for impact, these students reported more change than did any other samples with regard to feelings of self-confidence and independence, and also in the area of religious attitudes. They were second in frequency of mention of the impact on their intellectual development, but well below the average (tenth out of 11) with regard to personal changes.

(7) Iran. Foreign students included in the study (N = 73) were predominantly male (seven out of ten) and came mainly from countries in the Middle East and Afghanistan. They were involved in various disciplines, with four out of ten indicating "others"—with, as a consequence, relatively small proportions in the four areas usually considered as the major disciplinary concerns of foreign students. They reported least frequently among the 11 samples that they had been adequately or fairly well informed about the new environment before departure, and were second (after Japan) in complaining that even after arrival they had had difficulty in obtaining adequate information.

They were somewhat below average in being satisfied or very satisfied with their academic experience, and they were the lowest of all in satisfaction with their overall general and social experience at the university. They complained least often of difficulty with the local language, were second lowest with regard to difficulties in dealing with the university administration, and third lowest in reporting a lack of personal counseling. They were about average as regards problems with examinations, and in complaints about insufficient previous training. They were above the average with regard to difficulty in adjusting to local food, in relations with the opposite sex, and in lacking information regarding progress in studies; below average in reporting personal depression, and problems of contact with local students and the general population. With regard to housing, their complaints about expense were relatively rare, but they felt the lack of personal privacy, of comfort and cleanliness more than the majority of other samples. They ranked finances, lack of facilities for recreation and sports, and difficulties in dealing with the local administration as their most troublesome problems.

Their judgments regarding the teaching staff were the most severe of all samples with reference to the intellectual stimulation provided and the helpfulness of teachers in general. With regard to the accessibility of teachers, their judgment was more severe than for most other samples, but was exceeded by the foreign students in France and equaled by those in Japan. Only with regard to the teaching quality in general was their reaction relatively favorable.

As for contact, they were the least likely to report that they were rooming with a local student, and among the least frequent to mention that they had made good friends since their arrival (only the students in France showed a lower proportion in this respect, although the percentages were fairly high in both cases). They were below average in reporting that contact was usually with a local student, and about average in having a local student as "best friend." They were close to the average also in their comments on opportunities for social contact with Iranians or visits to local families, but much less likely (only the students in Japan were less likely than they) to report having positive contacts with people in the neighborhood or sharing meals with them.

In the area of international relations, these students were close to the average (one in four) in feeling that the local population had a reasonably accurate knowledge of their (the foreign students') country and above average in judging that the attitude of the local people was favorable or very favorable. They themselves started out with a somewhat better than average opinion of Iranians, and ended up feeling less favorable, but definitely more favorable than the average of the 11 samples. About one student in four (only Brazil showed a smaller percentage) reported that friends or relatives had suffered discrimination, and about one in five (well below the average) that they had had that experience themselves. About one in seven (close to the average) expressed the desire to stay in Iran if that were possible. Three out of ten (the lowest proportion of the 11 samples) stated that they had become more positive about their own country, and six out of ten (the largest percentage) that the sojourn had no effect in this connection.

Regarding the general impact of the sojourn, the students in Iran were the least likely of all to report changes in their personal and social development or in feelings of independence, and only in Hong Kong were the students less likely than those in Iran to indicate changes in feelings of self-confidence. They were also the least likely to indicate that the experience had opened up new research interests, ideas, and opportunities, although there were still close to seven out of ten who answered this question affirmatively.

(8) Japan. Foreign students in Japan constitute the smallest of our national samples (N = 30), and the caution we expressed regarding the generalization of our findings in the cases of the Federal Republic

of Germany and Hong Kong also applies in this case. The students
were two-thirds male, and came mainly from other Asian countries,
particularly Taiwan and Korea. The disciplines represented were
primarily engineering-physical sciences and arts-humanities.

They reported less frequently than did the majority of those in
the 11 country samples that before leaving they had received fair-to-
adequate information regarding their foreign sojourn, and the smallest minority of all felt that the information received after arrival
was adequate for their purposes. They were second lowest in feeling satisfied or very satisfied with their overall academic experience,
but above average in satisfaction with their general and social experience.

With regard to problems and difficulties, they complained the
least frequently of all the country samples of experiencing personal
depression and having difficulty in adjusting to the local food and
climate, and they were second lowest in complaining about relations
with the opposite sex and lack of contact with local people. They
were also below average in reporting difficulties in dealing with the
university administration, problems of equivalence or proper placement level, and finances. On the other hand, they were second highest in complaints about the difficulty of courses and (exceeded only
by the experience in France) lack of contact with local fellow students (in spite of infrequent complaints regarding the difficulty of
contact with the general population). They were well above average
in reporting that they had received too little information regarding
their progress in their studies, and in having problems with examinations. They were also somewhat above average regarding
lack of framework and direction in their academic program, insufficient previous training, and lack of counseling. As for housing,
they complained frequently (exceeded only by France) of its excessive expense, and also of the lack of available housing and of the
distance from the university. They were lowest of all in mentioning
difficulties with local transportation, or lack of cleanliness (not a
single complaint), and relatively rarely spoke of any lack of general
comfort. Their most troublesome difficulties were finances and
lack of framework and direction in their academic program.

Their rating of teachers was relatively rather low. With regard to helpfulness and teaching qualities, the absolute ratings remained positive, although well below the average of the other country samples. In the case of intellectual stimulation and accessibility
of the majority of teachers, the judgment dropped to neutral. As for
intellectual stimulation, the figure in Japan was equaled by that in
Hong Kong, and was more negative in Iran; for accessibility, the
Japanese figure equaled that in Iran, and was more negative only in
France.

Regarding social contacts, these students were above average in reporting that they had made good friends since arrival, and that their best friend was likely to be a local student. On the other hand, their contacts were most likely to be with fellow nationals (exceeded in this respect only by students in Iran). They were above average in reported opportunities for social contact with local families and in invitations to visit their homes, and yet least likely of all in terms of frequency of contacts with neighbors or eating meals with them. (This seeming contradiction can be explained by the living arrangements for foreign students at this particular Japanese university.)

Only one out of five of these students felt that the Japanese had a reasonably accurate knowledge of their (the foreign students') country, or that their attitude was favorable. In no case was this attitude judged to be very favorable. In both of these judgments, the students in Japan were well below the average. Their opinion of the Japanese when they arrived was the lowest of all the country samples (although still positive in absolute terms) and improved slightly by the time the investigation was conducted. A majority (the largest proportion of all the samples) reported that their friends or relatives had encountered discrimination in Japan; a somewhat smaller percentage, but still the largest of all the samples, stated that they themselves had had a similar experience. About one foreign student in seven (well below average) would like to stay in Japan if possible. They were above average in reporting that their stay abroad had made them more positive about their own country, and only in very rare cases more negative.

Regarding the general impact, they were well above average in estimating substantial change in their personal development, their feelings of self-confidence and independence, but they were below average in their estimate of much change in intellectual terms. Eight out of ten (about average) reported that the sojourn had opened up new research ideas or interests for them.

(9) Kenya. Foreign students questioned in Kenya numbered 84, mainly from other African countries, particularly Uganda and secondly Tanzania, and three out of four were males. Their academic disciplines varied greatly, with approximately one-third in the category of "others," but with about one-fourth in engineering-physical sciences.

In general, they were definitely above average in judging that they were fairly well or adequately informed before attending the foreign university, and were the most frequent to state that the information they received after arrival was quite adequate. Their assessment of their academic experience was also well above average, as was their satisfaction with the overall general and social aspects. Their satisfaction was high both relatively and absolutely.

As for problems and difficulties, they complained most frequently (by far) of lack of a private place to study, problems of equivalence or proper placement, finances, relations with the opposite sex, and also of lack of personal counseling and difficulties with the local language. They were in second place with regard to lack of information regarding progress in their studies, and above the average in reporting difficulties in dealing with the university administration. They were below average in reporting lack of contact with the general population or local students, problems with examinations, insufficient previous training, the climate, and personal depression. They were above average with regard to complaints about local food, and difficulty of courses. They were the least frequent of all to complain about lack of framework and direction in their academic program. With regard to housing, they complained by far most frequently of all about lack of personal privacy, the difficulty of finding available housing, and the lack of cleanliness, but they were less concerned than the average with the excessive expense involved. They listed as their main problems the lack of a private place in which to study and the question of equivalence or proper placement on arrival.

Their reactions to the teachers were in general favorable. They were the most satisfied of all the samples in the judgment of teaching quality and the intellectual stimulation provided, and well above average with regard to their accessibility and helpfulness. It may very well be that the university in Kenya impressed them as being definitely superior in most cases to those with which these foreign students were familiar.

As for contact, they were the most frequent of all to state that they had made good friends since arrival (almost the total sample in Kenya) and second in frequency of having a local student as a roommate (exceeded only by Hong Kong) and in indicating that their social contact was mainly with local students (with West Germany first). Their "best friend" was, however, more likely to be a fellow national than a local student. They were the most frequent to report positive contacts with neighbors and to have meals with them; they were average in terms of contact with local families but above average in invitations to visit such families.

They were the most frequent (together with foreign students in West Germany) to find that the local population had a reasonably accurate knowledge of their (the foreign students') own countries, but were surprisingly the least frequent to judge the local attitude as favorable or very favorable; more than half found it to be unfavorable or very unfavorable. As for discrimination, three in ten reported that their friends or relatives had had that experience, and a somewhat larger proportion (about one-third) said that they themselves had encountered discrimination. (These figures are fairly close to the average of all 11 country samples.) Their opinion of Kenya was favorable to start with, in fact the most favorable of all, and became even more positive as a consequence of the sojourn. On the other hand, the smallest proportion of all (about one in ten) wished to remain in the country; we have no explanation of this apparent paradox. Also, the largest proportion of all now felt more positive about their own country (close to one-half), and the smallest proportion (one in 20) felt more negative.

The students were most frequent of all to judge their experience as having effected changes in their personal and intellectual development, and second (to India) in reporting changes in their feelings of self-confidence. On the other hand, they were very unlikely to report new research interests, ideas, or opportunities as a consequence (only Iran reported less change in this respect).

(10) The United Kingdom. The sample in the United Kingdom (N = 370) was about two-thirds male, and about equally distributed in the engineering-physical sciences, the arts-humanities, and the behavioral-social sciences. They came mainly from countries that are at present or were formerly within the British Commonwealth, but the largest single group came from the United States.

They were the most likely of all the samples to indicate that they had received fair or adequate information before arrival, and second in finding such information readily available and adequate after they had arrived. They were the most likely of all to state that they were satisfied or very satisfied with their academic experience, and well above average with regard to their general and social experience. Satisfaction was high in both absolute and relative terms. As for difficulties, these students were the least likely to complain about the problem of dealing with the university administration, or the problem of establishing equivalences or proper placement levels. They were second to last in frequency of complaints regarding lack of a private place to study, problems with examinations, language, and finances, and third to last in reporting lack of contact with local students, lack of facilities for recreation and sports, or difficulties with the opposite sex. In other respects, they were at or near the average. As regards housing, they were less likely than the average to complain of difficulty in finding adequate housing, of lack of personal privacy, or of general comfort. Their most troublesome problems were finances and personal depression, although in these two areas their frequency of complaints was about average.

Their experience with the teaching staff was favorable. They were first in frequency of appreciation of the helpfulness of teachers, second with regard to their intellectual stimulation, and (together with students in Brazil and Canada) second also as regards their accessibility. They were fourth (together once more with Canada) regarding the teaching quality in general.

With regard to social contacts, they were third in reporting that their best friend in the country was a local student, and above average in stating that their main contact was with local students, that they had a local student as a roommate, and that they had made good friends since arrival. They were above average also in having opportunities for social contact with local families, in receiving invitations to visit them, to have positive contacts with people in their neighborhood, and to have meals with them.

They were above average in finding that local people had a reasonably accurate knowledge of their (the foreign students') countries, and close to the average in judging the attitude to be favorable or very favorable. They started out (in third place) with a relatively positive opinion regarding the local population and that opinion deteriorated slightly, but still remained in third place by the time of the investigation. They were below average in the frequency of reported discrimination against friends or relatives, and well below the average (about one in five) in reporting discrimination against themselves. They were close to the average (about one in seven) to express the desire to remain in the United Kingdom, but well below in feeling more positive about their own country as a result of the foreign sojourn.

As for impact, they were more likely than the average to report the opening up of new research ideas and interests and also that there had been changes in their personal development. They were less likely than the average to report changes in their intellectual development, their feelings of independence, and self-confidence.

(11) The United States. This sample of foreign students was the largest (N = 955), predominantly male (approximately four out of five) and coming from a wide variety of countries, with the largest single groups from India, Taiwan, Iran, Thailand, the United Kingdom, and Canada. Their principal disciplinary identity was with engineering-physical sciences (almost half) and secondly the behavioral-social sciences. They were well above average in indicating that they had received fair or adequate information before arrival, and in stating that since arriving the available information was adequate.

They were also well above average in stating they were satisfied or very satisfied both with their academic and general social and nonacademic experience at the university. They complained rather more than the average of problems with examinations, the difficulty of courses, lack of a private place to study, and finances; about average regarding lack of contact with local people or students, food, language, and relations with the opposite sex; below average as to insufficient previous training, dealing with the university administration, climate, and lack of counseling; the least, or close to the least, regarding equivalences or proper placement on arrival, lack of information regarding progress in studies, lack of facilities for recreation and sports, and absence of framework and direction in academic programs. As for lodging, they complained more than the average about the excessive expense and difficulties with local transportation, and less than the average regarding lack of personal privacy, distance from the university, and lack of cleanliness or general comfort. Their most troublesome problems related to finances, local food, and climate.

As for experience with the teaching staff, they were the most satisfied of all the country samples with the accessibility of the majority of teachers, in second place (after the United Kingdom) as to their helpfulness, and third with regard to the teaching quality in general and the intellectual stimulation provided. With regard to accessibility, in which foreign students in the United States were highest and those in France the lowest, we obtain confirmation of a widespread judgment regarding American and French professors respectively. One of the authors of this report has been teaching in France for more than 15 years and previously taught at an American university for more than 30. His judgment, shared by many colleagues familiar with both academic systems, fits in perfectly with this finding. French professors are, however, very accessible to advanced students.

In the area of contact, foreign students in the United States were about average (but close to nine out of ten) in reporting that they had made good friends since arrival, and more likely than the average to state that their best friend in the country was a local student, that their roommate in the majority of cases was a local student, and that their contacts with others were likely (also in the majority of cases) to be with a local student. They were above average in reporting opportunities for contact with local families and invitations to visit them, and about average in terms of positive contacts with neighbors or sharing meals with them. They relatively rarely (second to Brazil, which was lowest in this respect) felt that the local population had a reasonably accurate knowledge of their (the foreign students') country, and were somewhat below average in judging their attitude to be favorable or very favorable. They were close to the average in reporting that their friends or relatives had experienced discrimination and that they themselves had had that experience. Their opinion of the local population, although generally favorable, was less so than in the case of other groups on arrival, and became very slightly less favorable during the course of the sojourn. They were a little below average in the frequency with which they expressed the desire to remain in the country of sojourn. About one in three (close to the average) stated that they had become more positive about their own country.

They were above average in feeling that their experience had opened up new research ideas or opportunities, and that changes had occurred in their intellectual development and feelings of independence, and below average in the frequency of reporting changes in personal development or feelings of self-confidence.

11

INTERNATIONAL
INTERRELATIONSHIPS

So far in these discussions, both so-called "hard data" from pen and pencil instruments completed by respondents in 11 participating countries and "soft data" from longitudinal interviews with newly arriving foreign students throughout their initial year have been presented and considered. In most cases, the statistical data have both complemented and supported that which was evident in the interview data and vice versa. In any investigation, both types of data are necessary in order to arrive at a picture that can be viewed as fair. Still, throughout these discussions we have focused primarily on foreign students in one country compared with others among the 11 participating countries as well as on particular variables or items either of interest in themselves or because they were felt to be relevant to previous research hypotheses or assumptions. We now approach the data from a different perspective, one that appears to us as being both intriguing and controversial.

As the data in this investigation have shown, it is clear that students from one country differ in many respects from those from other countries. This is especially true when the particular countries are vastly different in terms of size, personal wealth, standards of living, educational systems, and so on. Indeed, it has frequently been argued that there is no such thing as "the foreign student." Students have to be considered in terms of various differences, especially geographic origin, and cannot be lumped together under a single category. The very number of significant differences that have been pointed out in the previous chapters with regard to the geographical origin of respondents supports this conclusion.

It is, however, also reasonable and very important to consider those common factors that seem to operate for foreign students regardless of where they are studying or from where they come. If there are experiences, problems, or attitudes that foreign students commonly express, then these need to be known. Such knowledge is crucial if we are to understand international exchange from a global perspective.

In view of all the data that were collected during this present investigation, it would be an impossible task to intercorrelate everything. Decisions had to be taken to select the data which appeared to be most interesting and potentially illuminating both in view of past research as well as in relation to present and possibly future discussions of international exchange. With this in mind, a series of variables were identified for study that could be viewed internationally.

DATA VARIABLES FOR INTERNATIONAL ANALYSES

The following variables were selected for cross tabulation analyses:

1. Traveled versus untraveled: Two items from the instrument were combined to form this variable:

Have you previously visited this country for more than one month BEFORE your present stay?

Have you visited any other foreign countries for continuous periods of more than one month?

Respondents who replied "no" to both items were considered to be "untraveled" prior to their present sojourn experience. Respondents who replied "yes" to either item were considered to be "traveled." The variable thus distinguished between those who had previously been in any foreign country for periods of more than one month prior to their present sojourn and those who had not been to other countries for more than one month, and who could thus be considered to be less experienced, if not inexperienced, in terms of international travel and the adjustments and problems that usually accompany such travel. Previous experience in a foreign country could be expected to influence the coping process of a student in a host country. Whether such experience can be gained in the space of one month, as the variable assumed, is a question with minimal previous support[1] but is certainly worth further investigation.

2. Nationality of others when in the company of others:

When you are in the company of others, are they mainly:

(a) local (country)* students.
(b) fellow nationals (students).
(c) other foreign students.
(d) local (country) non-students.
(e) a (country) family.
(f) other, please specify.

Options "a," "d," and "e," all referring to local people, were combined. Option "f" was deleted as were omit responses. The resulting divisions distinguished between those reporting their company to be mainly with local people, in contrast to the company of fellow nationals or other foreign students.

3. Nationality of the "best friend" in the host country:

Specify the nationality of your best friend in this country:

(a) local (country) student.
(b) fellow national (student).
(c) other foreign student.
(d) local (country) non-student.
(e) a (country) family.

Combinations were made as above (Point 2), giving resulting divisions between those reporting that their "best friend" in the host country was a local individual or family, a fellow national, or another foreign student.

4. Contact with local individuals: A series of items was utilized here:

Do you have opportunities for social contact with (country) families?

Have you ever been invited to visit (country) families?

Do you go for walks, outings, or evenings with (country)?

Do you do academic work in cooperation with (country)?

Are you involved in community activities with (country)?

---

*Throughout, the form "(country)" is used in quoting items to indicate that the name of the people where the instruments were being completed was inserted. For example, the option might read, "local Indian students," "local American students," "an Iranian family," "a Kenyan family," and so on.

Are you collaborating on an artistic function or social function with (country)? (theatrical performance, film club, or social action).

Do you have the opportunity to discuss what you consider to be significant issues with (country)?

Do you have positive contacts with neighbors at your apartment, hotel, pension, etc.?

Do you have meals with (country) in your neighborhood?

Respondents replied in terms of "very often," "often," "sometimes," "rarely," or "never," with value scores assigned of 1 through 5. The total score for each respondent was calculated and used for this variable.

5. "Lots of contact" or "medium contact" or "little contact" with local individuals: The identical items used above (Point 4) were grouped in the following divisions:

	Mean	St. Dev.	N	Percent	Total Score
"Lots of contact"	18.06	3.47	473	20	22 or below
"Medium contact"	29.66	3.87	1409	60	23 through 36
"Little contact"	39.74	2.36	462	20	37 or above

While these divisions are arbitrary and are characterized only by the total score of respondents on the particular items used in this investigation, they did permit comparisons between those respondents reporting more and less contact respectively with local individuals.

6. Person with whom lodging is shared: Respondents were asked to identify with which of the following they were sharing lodging if they were sharing lodging:

—my spouse.
—local (country) students.
—fellow nationals (students).
—other foreign students.
—local (country) non-students.
—a (country) family.
—other, please specify.

Each option offered a "yes" or "no" response. Combinations were
again made on the basis of sharing lodging with locals, fellow nationals, or other foreign students exclusively (as explained in Point
2 above). Those living alone were of course excluded.

7. Difficulties and problems: Respondents were asked to identify
any problems or difficulties they were having by checking those items
on the following list that were a source of difficulty at the moment or
in the past that affected their stay in the sojourn country:

—financial problems.
—ill health.
—personal depression.
—difficulty adjusting to climate.
—difficulty adjusting to local food.
—difficulty with the local language.
—lack of opportunity to use the local language.
—relations with the opposite sex.
—problems relating to religion.
—lack of framework and direction in academic program.
—lack of personal counseling.
—lack of contact with fellow students.
—lack of contact with local people.
—lack of motivation in my studies.
—lack of facilities for recreation and sports.
—lack of a private place to study.
—problems with examinations.
—difficulty of courses.
—lack of information regarding progress in studies.
—difficulties in dealing with the university administration.
—insufficient previous training.
—problems of equivalence or proper placement upon arrival.
—a change in your objectives.
—other, please specify.

The total number of problems checked minus the last option, "other,"
which was not included in this analysis, resulted in a ranking not
only of problem areas but also of the total number of problems or
difficult areas that was reported by individual respondents.

8. "Many," "some," or "few" problems or difficulties: Using the
same check list presented above (Point 7), respondents were grouped
in the following divisions:

	Mean	St. Dev.	N	Percent	Total Score
"Many difficulties"	9.26	3.23	454	18	7 or above
"Some difficulties"	3.62	1.37	1521	61	2 through 6
"Few difficulties"	0.63	0.48	539	21	1 or zero

Again, the divisions were arbitrary, but they permitted comparisons between those reporting more and fewer difficulties and sources of problems respectively, during their sojourns.

9. Personal depression: Specific attention was directed to those respondents who identified "personal depression" in the above list (Point 7) of sources of difficulty. As was determined during the pilot testing of the items, foreign student respondents viewed this category as indicating a severe and serious problem of a personal nature. One can only assume that the same meaning was attached to the item during the international data collection.

10. Personal discrimination:

Have you personally had the experience of being discriminated against in this country?

Respondents were asked to reply either "yes" or "no." Omits were not included in this variable.

11. Opinion regarding the local people:

What is your opinion of the (country) people today?

(a) very favorable
(b) favorable
(c) neutral
(d) unfavorable
(e) very unfavorable

12. Loneliness:

Do you feel lonely here?

(a) very often
(b) often

(c) sometimes
(d) rarely
(e) never

13. Homesickness:

Do you feel homesick here?

(a) very often
(b) often
(c) sometimes
(d) rarely
(e) never

14. Teaching quality in general:

In terms of your own personal experience with the teaching staff, how do you rate the following:

—the teaching quality in general.

Responses were in terms of "very satisfactory," "satisfactory," "neutral," "unsatisfactory," "very unsatisfactory," and "no comment/not applicable." The "no comment/not applicable" and omit responses were not used for the variable.

15. Helpfulness of teachers in general:

In terms of your own personal experience with the teaching staff, how do you rate the following:

—the helpfulness of teachers in general.

The same combinations were used here as for the variable immediately above (Point 14).

16. Impact of the sojourn: Respondents were asked to assess the impact of their sojourn as follows:

The following questions relate to your evaluation of your study experience abroad so far. As a result of your experience living in this country, how much have you changed in regard to the following areas?

—your personal development?
—your intellectual development?
—your political opinions?
—your religious attitudes?

—your feeling of self-confidence?
—your feeling of independence?

Respondents were asked to reply to each segment on the basis of "very much," "much," "I am not sure," "little," "very little," or "none." Using a value score of 1 through 6, a total score was calculated for each respondent and used for this variable.

17. "High," "medium," or "low" impact of the sojourn: Using the same items as presented above (Point 16), respondents were grouped in the following divisions:

	Mean	St. Dev.	N	Percent	Total Score
"High impact"	10.91	2.03	498	20.99	13 or below
"Medium impact"	17.99	2.70	1386	58.41	14 through 23
"Low impact"	27.93	3.37	489	20.60	24 or above

As in the case of other grouped data, these divisions are arbitrary, and they are used here only for the purpose of comparisons between groups of respondents who report having experienced relatively more or less change in themselves as a result of their experience in the sojourn country.

18. Geographic origin: The difficulties with any variable dealing with the origin of respondents have been dealt with in some detail earlier (Chapter 3). The geographic area divisions used in this variable for the purposes of cross tabulations of data were the following:

Western Europe,
United Kingdom,
Eastern Europe,
black Africa,
Arabic-speaking countries,
Iran,
South Pacific countries,
South Asia,
South East Asia,
other Asian countries,
Latin America,
Canada,
United States.

A complete listing of each country included within the above geographic divisions is found in Appendix C.

19. <u>Overall satisfaction with studies</u>: In order to obtain evaluative data in terms of how respondents viewed their sojourns with regard to the academic and nonacademic aspects, two specific items were placed at the end of the instrument (see also Point 10):

In general, how do you feel about your overall experience in this country with regard to the following two areas?

With general regard to my studies, I feel:

(a) very satisfied.
(b) satisfied.
(c) neutral.
(d) dissatisfied.
(e) very dissatisfied.

With general regard to other aspects of my experience abroad, I feel:

(a) very satisfied.
(b) satisfied.
(c) neutral.
(d) dissatisfied.
(e) very dissatisfied.

20. <u>Overall satisfaction with other (nonacademic) aspects of the sojourn</u>: The variable here focused on nonacademic aspects of the sojourn experience as viewed by the student (see Point 19 for the item's wording). This item with the exception of an additional page for respondents to make suggestions that might improve the situation for other foreign students, completed the instrument.

CROSS TABULATION ANALYSES

Each of the above 20 variables (Points 1 through 20) was cross tabulated with each of the remaining 19. The presence or absence of significant relationships among the data in these analyses is shown in Table 11.1.

It should be noted that in every case where items are mentioned as significant, such relationships are at or beyond the .01 level. That is to say, the Type I error was set at .01 throughout this investigation and for all data reported in this book.

TABLE 11.1

Cross Tabulation Variables

	1	2	3	4	5	6	7	8	9	10	11	12	13	14	15	16	17	18	19	20
1. "Traveled" vs. "untraveled"	-																			
2. Nationality of others when in the company of others	*	-																		
3. Nationality of the "best friend" in the host country	*	*	-																	
4. Contact with local individuals	*	*	*	-																
5. "Lots" vs. "medium" vs. "little" contact with local individuals	*	*	*	-	-															
6. Persons with whom lodging is shared	*	*	*	*	*	-														
7. Difficulties and problems	*	*	*	*	*	*	-													
8. "Many" vs. "some" vs. "few" difficulties and problems					*	*	-	-												
9. Personal depression					*	*	*	-	-											
10. Personal discrimination					*	*	*	*	-	-										
11. Opinion of the local people					*	*	*	*	*	-	-									
12. Loneliness					*	*	*	*	*	*	*	-								
13. Homesickness					*	*	*	*	*	*	*	*	-							
14. Teaching quality in general					*	*	*	*	*	*	*	*	*	-						
15. Helpfulness of teachers in general					*	*	*	*	*	*	*	*	*	*	-					
16. Impact from the sojourn					*	*	*	*	*	*	*	*	*	*	-	-				
17. "High" vs. "medium" vs. "low" impact from the sojourn					*	*	*	*	*	*	*	*	*	*	*	-	-			
18. Geographic origin	*	*	*	*	*	*	*	*	*	*	*	*	*	*	*	*	-	-		
19. Overall satisfaction with studies		*	*	*	*	*	*	*	*	*	*	*	*	*	*	*	*	*	-	
20. Overall satisfaction with other (non-academic) aspects of the sojourn		*	*	*	*	*	*	*	*	*	*	*	*	*	*	*	*	*	-	-
	1	2	3	4	5	6	7	8	9	10	11	12	13	14	15	16	17	18	19	20

*Significant at the .01 level.

Source: Compiled by the authors.

DISCUSSION OF THE RESULTS

Rather than presenting each significant relationship located within the cross tabulation analyses and discussing the direction of each relationship, it seems more appropriate to offer a less technical discussion with more attention given to implications from the results in terms of the various assumptions and factors generally discussed with regard to international educational exchange. Such a presentation is bound to disappoint the more technical reader but may serve to stimulate the thinking of those who are responsible for policy decisions and day-to-day operations of international educational exchange. A great deal could have been written on each of the variables, but we have limited our comments to some of the more interesting results, especially those with implications for policy formation.

(1) "Traveled" versus "untraveled" respondents: There does seem to be a clear relationship between previous travel and the sojourn experience in terms of various types of social contact between foreign students and local people. Those who had traveled were not only more likely to report that they were mainly with local students and non-students when they were with others, but were also more likely to identify a local person as their "best friend" in the sojourn country and to have a local student (if they did not have a spouse) as a roommate. Conversely, those who were untraveled more frequently reported spending their time with fellow nationals, named a fellow national as their "best friend," and shared lodging with a fellow national.

Those more experienced in travel and in adjusting to foreign cultures did have a distinctly different experience, at least in the initial stages of the sojourn and with local people, as compared with those who left their home countries for the first time to a strange land. The experiences of these latter students are, of course, included in the case study interviews that were a part of this international investigation and have been presented in Chapter 10.

(2) Nationality of others when in the company of others: It is commonly said that a great deal can be told from the company one keeps. In terms of the foreign students in this investigation, that seemed to be true. Those spending time mainly with local students, non-students, or families were the most likely to have a local student as a "best friend" and as a person with whom lodging was shared. They were the least likely to indicate that they had a problem with "personal depression" or personal discrimination in the sojourn country. They had more favorable opinions regarding the local people and

were the least likely to report loneliness or homesickness. Furthermore, they were likely to rate more highly the helpfulness of teachers at the sojourn institutions.

The converse was true for those reporting that they spent
their time primarily with fellow national or other foreign students.

(3) Nationality of the "best friend" in the host country: Those foreign students reporting a local student as a "best friend" were not
only more likely to be sharing lodging with a local student, but were
also less likely to indicate personal depression, and to report the
personal experience of discrimination. They reported loneliness
and homesickness with less frequency. They were also more satisfied with the teaching quality at the host university and rated the
helpfulness of faculty more highly.

(4 and 5) Contact with local individuals as well as "high" and "low"
contact groups: As might be anticipated, both analyses produced almost identical results.

As might be expected, those with higher contact with local
people were most likely to report that their "best friend" as well as
the person with whom they were sharing lodging were local people.
They were most likely not to have reported personal depression or to
have been discriminated against in the host country. Their opinion
of the local people was more favorable, they reported being lonely
and homesick less often, were more pleased with the teaching quality and staff, and were, in general, more satisfied with both academic
and nonacademic aspects of their sojourn. Those whose contact was
primarily with fellow nationals or other foreign students gave results
in the opposite direction on the above items.

In the light of these data, it appears reasonable to stress the
importance of contact with local people for foreign students in general, but we will have more to say about this when we reconsider
the modified culture contact hypothesis later.

(6) Person with whom lodging is shared: Since contact with local
people is an important variable in terms of significant relationships
with other items in this investigation of the coping and adaptation
processes, it might be expected that a crucial factor might be a
local roommate. This was the case in our data.

Significant results with regard to the "roommate" indicated
that those living with a spouse or local student were less likely to
report personal depression, while those living with other foreign
students were the most likely to do so. Furthermore, those living
with a spouse or local student were less likely to indicate loneliness;
those living with other foreign students were more likely to do so.

The comparatively smaller number of significant relationships for this variable contrasts markedly with the large number that were reported above with regard to the other contact variables (see Points 2, 3, 4, 5, above). This may indicate that actually living with a local individual in the foreign setting is not so important as access to local individuals in terms of perceived sojourn satisfaction and the coping and adaptation processes.

It should also be noted that the presence of a spouse or living with the foreign student did appear to be a positive factor. As some of the case studies indicate, spouses can contribute positively to the foreign student's life and work if that spouse is contented and happy. However, a frustrated spouse, incapable or afraid of interaction with the local language, people, or culture, can indeed make things very difficult.

Our correlations indicate that the person with whom one shares a residence may not be the most important factor at the sojourn location in terms of the overall coping and adaptation processes. This finding argues against those who feel it is of crucial importance for the foreign student to have a local student roommate. Our data would rather suggest, as already indicated, that access to local people (amount of contact and kinds of contact) is more important than sharing residence with a local student.

(7 and 8) Difficulties and problems as well as "many" or "few" problems: As was the case in other analyses where respondents were grouped for further study as well as considered on the basis of total, individual scores, both analyses of this variable produced almost identical results. The foreign students who reported "few" difficulties in the sojourn situation tended also to be those who were primarily with local students or non-students when they were with others, and had named a local student or non-student as their "best friend." Their lodging was shared with a spouse or a local student. They were less likely to check personal depression as a problem nor to report personal discrimination. These respondents with "few" difficulties also reported a more favorable opinion with regard to the local people, were less frequently lonely and homesick, rated the quality of the teachers and their helpfulness more favorably, and were more satisfied both academically and nonacademically with their sojourn experiences at the point of this investigation.

Again, it is important to note that the foreign students who could be characterized by having "fewer" difficulties or problems were also significantly more likely to report more contact with local students or non-students, in terms of spending time with them, in contrast to those whose contact was primarily with fellow nationals or other foreign students.

(9) Personal depression: As was mentioned earlier, the occurrence of "personal depression" in a foreign student is a complex, difficult, and serious matter. Having concluded from the pilot investigations that students interpreted this item to refer to a serious personal problem that was both troublesome and debilitating in some ways and a problem for which some outside assistance would be appropriate, we felt that the item itself is worthy of careful study.

Personal depression was checked as a problem by 21.5 percent of the total population responding to the check list international-ly as well as specified by 4 percent as "the most troublesome area" for them. The latter figure is, however, unrealistically low since there were a large number of respondents who neglected to specify "the most troublesome area" of their sojourn even though they re-sponded to the check list itself.

The country samples showed the following percentages of per-sonal depression:

Country	Percent
Brazil	32.2
India	30.4
Canada	24.5
France	21.9
Hong Kong	21.4
United Kingdom	20.8
United States	19.4
Kenya	16.7
Iran	15.1
Federal Republic of Germany	11.9
Japan	6.7

What is important to note here is that the significant relation-ships in the data for those checking personal depression do not offer any clear direction either for identifying such individuals or altering their situation. Those checking personal depression were, among other things:

- more likely to indicate that they felt themselves the object of per-sonal discrimination in the sojourn country.
- more likely to report a less favorable opinion regarding the local people at the point of this research.
- more likely to report loneliness and homesickness.
- more likely to report having found the helpfulness of teachers at the sojourn institutions to be less satisfactory.

Social contact with local people, as has already been pointed out, was significantly related to the absence of personal depression, as was spending time in the company of local students and having a local student as a "best friend" in the sojourn country.

(10) Personal discrimination: The perception of personal discrimination on the part of a foreign student, whether or not such discrimination could be established as having occurred as an objective fact, was related to various aspects of the sojourn experience. Those respondents who reported personal discrimination also reported a less favorable opinion concerning the local people, were lonely and homesick more frequently, and held a lower opinion of the teaching quality and helpfulness of the teachers at the sojourn institution (in addition to the relationships that have already been noted in this chapter).

(11) Opinion concerning the local people: Those variables that were significantly related to a less favorable opinion of the local people were also related to the perception of personal discrimination (Point 10). In addition, those respondents with a less favorable opinion of the local people reported loneliness and homesickness more frequently and held a lower opinion of the teaching quality and helpfulness of the teachers at the sojourn institutions. The relationship between these two variables and with other variables related to social contact and assessment of the sojourn were as anticipated and are mentioned throughout this chapter.

(12 and 13) Loneliness and homesickness: These variables were highly related to each other and to the presence or absence of social contact and relationships with local individuals in the anticipated directions. That is to say that greater social contact and more involvement with local students were correlated with the absence of loneliness and homesickness.

(14) Teaching quality in general: The assessment of teaching quality as positive was also related to greater social contact with local people and more involvement with local students. The variable was also related to a more positive assessment of the academic and non-academic aspects of the sojourn experience in general. It was also positively correlated with the variable of helpfulness of teachers in general.

(15) Helpfulness of teachers in general: Significant correlations with regard to this variable were, in general, what might be anticipated

in terms of the results of the above analyses. Those respondents who did not report negative experiences, perceptions, or attitudes were more likely to report that the teachers at the host institution were most helpful to them. For example, those who did not report personal depression or the personal experience of discrimination, who were lonely and homesick less frequently, who were more satisfied with the academic and nonacademic aspects of their sojourn experiences, and who had the more favorable opinions with regard to the local people were the most likely to rate the helpfulness of their teachers as very satisfactory. Such respondents also were the most likely to indicate that when they were with others, the others were mainly local students (in contrast to those who were with fellow nationals and who viewed the helpfulness of teachers as unsatisfactory or neutral, or those who were with other foreign students who viewed the helpfulness of their teachers as very unsatisfactory). These respondents were the most likely to name a local student as their "best friend" in the sojourn country and to show significantly more social contact with local people than those who were more dissatisfied with the helpfulness of their teachers.

As was mentioned above (Point 14), the results were in the same direction for the assessment of the quality of teaching at the host institutions.

(16 and 17) Amount and character of impact: The data from these analyses did provide a number of interesting relationships.

Those who reported personal depression as well as those who reported personal discrimination were more likely to be in the high impact group. Furthermore, while neither the type of individuals in whose company respondents reported spending their time nor the individual specified as the "best friend" was significantly related to either impact variable, the amount of social contact was related in that those who were in the "medium group" in terms of social contact were also in the "medium group" in terms of impact. High impact was significantly related to a more favorable opinion of the local people at the time of the research, to a higher rating of the teaching quality at the host institution, and to more satisfaction with both the overall academic as well as nonacademic aspects of the sojourn experience.

In other words, high impact perceptions were not related to high social contact or to contact with local or nonlocal individuals in terms of either spending time with them or considering one to be the "best friend." The relationship between experiencing personal depression or personal discrimination and impact may indicate merely that these experiences are of such an intensely personal nature that they influence and are reflected in judgments of personal impact from the sojourn experience. About the most that can be said from the present data is that the perception of high impact was positively related to more positive overall assessments of both academic and nonacademic aspects of the sojourn experiences. This is certainly not surprising.

(18) Geographic origin: All of the analyses with regard to the variable of geographic origin were significant in our data. While this is partly to be expected given the nature of the statistical analyses with a total of 13 different geographical categories, the directions of the significant differences are striking. As such, they indicate specific differences in the coping and adaptation processes internationally.

In terms of previous travel, an important variable for initial adaptability in a sojourn country, those respondents most likely to have traveled previously for periods of at least one month were from Latin American countries. At the other extreme, those least likely to have traveled were from Asia.

As for problems and difficulties, respondents most likely to be in the "high difficulties" group were from Latin America, with black Africa and the Asian countries ranking next. Those most likely to be in the "low difficulties" group were also from Latin America, followed by the Asian countries. The presence of respondents from these two areas at both extremes is due to the fact that students from these two continents were more likely to perceive or place themselves in the extreme categories, while the respondents from other countries were more likely to hold the average or middle position. This particular tendency occurred again and again, especially for the Latin American respondents and, at times, for those from Asian countries.

Personal depression was most likely to be reported as a problem by respondents from Asia and Latin America (also least likely to be reported as a problem by those from Latin America). Personal discrimination was also the most likely to have been perceived and reported in respondents from the Asian and black African countries. Loneliness was reported as most frequent among those from black African and Asian countries; homesickness was most prevalent among those students from the black African countries and Latin America.

Those most likely to report a very favorable opinion regarding the local population were from Latin America. Those most likely to report a very unfavorable opinion were from black African countries, South Asia, and Latin America.

The quality of instruction at the host institution was most likely to be rated as very satisfactory if the respondents were from Latin America, followed by those from the United States, the black

African countries, and Arabic-speaking countries. At the other extreme, respondents most likely to rate the teaching quality as very unsatisfactory were from the United States. However, those who were the most likely to rate the helpfulness of teachers as very satisfactory were from Western Europe and the United States. Those the most likely to rate the helpfulness of teachers as very unsatisfactory were from Arabic-speaking countries.

As for contact with local people, the respondents in the "high contact" group were most likely to be from Asia, then from Arabic-speaking countries. Those in the "low contact" group were the most likely to come from the United States, with Latin America ranking second. In all geographic categories, the majority of the respondents fall into the "medium contact" group. Those from Latin America, the United States, and Western Europe were the most likely to indicate that when they were in the company of others, the others were local students. Those in the company of fellow nationals were most likely to be from the Asian, Arabic-speaking, and black African countries. Those saying "other foreign students" were from Latin America and Asia.

The "best friend" in the sojourn country was most likely to be a local student if the respondent was from Latin America, the United States, and Western Europe, in that order. The "best friend" was most likely to be a fellow national if the respondent was from Asia or black African countries, in that order, or to be another foreign student if the respondent was from Asia.

Those sharing their place of lodging with a spouse were the most likely to be from Latin America, followed by those from Asia, the Arabic-speaking countries, and then the United States. Respondents rooming with local students were most likely to be from the black African countries, with Latin America in second place. Those who roomed with fellow nationals were most likely to come from the Asian countries, while those with other foreign students were most likely to be from Latin America, with Asian countries as number two.

In connection with the last three sets of analyses, it should be noted that in each case the respondents from the Asian countries were identifiable by their contact with either fellow nationals or with other foreign students. That is to say, they were the most likely to report that when they were with others, the others were mainly fellow nationals. Similarly, their "best friend" in the sojourn country and their roommate were most likely to be fellow nationals or other foreign students.

In terms of perceived impact from the experience of living in the sojourn country, those in the "high impact" group were the most likely to be from Latin America, with Western Europe and the

Arabic-speaking countries in second and third place. Those in the "low impact" group were most likely to be from the Asian countries, followed by Latin America. This again illustrates the tendency of respondents from Latin America to fall in the extreme categories on various variables. It is important to add that the majority of respondents from each geographical grouping were in the "medium impact" group. (The majority was smaller in the case of Latin America.)

Finally, in terms of overall academic and nonacademic satisfaction in the sojourn country, the following findings emerged: Those respondents most likely to be in the very satisfied category with regard to their studies were most likely to be from Latin America, followed by black Africa. Those most likely to be in the very dissatisfied category were most likely to be from the United States, with Latin America in second place. Those most likely to be in the very satisfied category with regard to the nonacademic aspects of their sojourns were most likely to be from the United States, followed by Latin America. Those most likely to be in the very dissatisfied category were most likely to be from South Asia or other countries in Asia.

We would suggest that the following points might be of special interest to those who deal with international educational exchange. First, students from the Asian countries are more likely to state that they spend their time predominantly with non-native students at the sojourn location. They are also more likely to report personal depression, personal discrimination, and loneliness. Even though they are more likely to be in frequent contact socially with native peoples, that contact does not seem to make them feel more comfortable with their sojourn or with the difficulties they perceive. In fact, those from the Asian countries together with those from South Asia were the most likely to report considerable dissatisfaction with the nonacademic aspects of their sojourn experience.

Second, students from the Latin American countries are the most likely to report their experiences and perceptions at one extreme or the other. They seem to feel that things either tend to go very well or very poorly for them.

Third, students from the Arabic-speaking countries are likely to have most of their contact in the company of other Arabic-speaking students. They are also the most likely to feel that the helpfulness of the teachers was very unsatisfactory; however, those from the United States are even more likely to be dissatisfied with the academic aspects of their sojourns.

Fourth, students from black Africa are likely to be having difficulties and problems during their sojourns. Their concerns, however, seem to be slightly less widespread or extreme than those presented by students from the Asian countries.

Fifth, one factor worth keeping in mind with regard to the coping and adjustment processes of students internationally is that those who may be expected to have difficulties—for example, those from Asia—may be viewed in terms of two specific groups: those with previous travel and adjustment experience and those without. Those with previous travel experience of more than four weeks in another foreign country will probably experience fewer difficulties and be less dissatisfied or upset by the coping and adaptation processes than those without.

Finally, it should be mentioned that the above generalizations are based, of course, on statistics and probability. There is a certain advantage in looking for generalizations, but these should never be permitted to lead to neglect of individual variations, especially in an area as complex as international student coping and adaptation.

(19) Overall satisfaction with studies: Those more satisfied with general regard to their studies in the sojourn country were also the most likely to be from Latin America, then black Africa, then Asia, and then the Arabic-speaking countries. Those most likely to be dissatisfied were from the United States, as was indicated above.

Those most satisfied reported medium amount of contact with local people, medium impact from the sojourn, and medium difficulties. They were most likely not to report personal depression or discrimination. They were also the most likely to be satisfied with the teaching quality and the helpfulness of the teachers. They reported a very favorable or favorable opinion regarding the local people. Those most satisfied with general regard to their studies were also most likely to indicate that when they were in the company of others, the others tended to be local students. While there was no significant difference in terms of the nationality of the roommate, those most satisfied with their studies were the most likely to specify that their "best friend" in the sojourn country was a local student.

(20) Overall satisfaction with other (nonacademic) aspects of the sojourn: Those who were very satisfied with the nonacademic aspects of their sojourn were most likely to be from the United States, Latin America, and Western Europe. Those least satisfied were most likely to be from either South Asia or Asia, with black Africa in third place.

Those most satisfied with the nonacademic aspects of their sojourn were the most likely not to report personal depression or personal discrimination, to be rarely or only sometimes lonely or homesick, and to feel satisfied with the teaching quality and teacher helpfulness at the host institutions. They were most likely to be in the "medium contact," "medium impact," and "medium problems or

difficulties" groupings. It is important to note that those who were
the least satisfied with the nonacademic aspects of their sojourns
were also the most likely to be in the high contact group (this seeming paradox will become clearer below). In other words, the individuals with the highest amounts of contact with local people were
not satisfied with the nonacademic aspects of their sojourns.

On the other hand, those most satisfied on this variable were
also those most likely to indicate that when they were in the company
of others, the others were local students (those who were least satisfied said that they were most likely to be in the company of other
foreign students). Furthermore, those most satisfied were also the
most likely to indicate that their "best friend" in the sojourn country
was a local student, while those least satisfied said that their "best
friend" was a fellow national student. In terms of the person with
whom lodging was being shared, those who were very satisfied were
the most likely to be sharing their lodging with a local student or,
secondly, with a spouse. Those least satisfied were the most likely
to be sharing lodgings with a spouse or fellow national student. Contact with local individuals thus appears to be important, but it is
clear that such contact can be too frequent, as in the case of the high
contact group. Contact with local individuals is necessary but it
does not need to be extreme in terms of frequency.

It is also worth noting that those who were satisfied with the
nonacademic aspects of their sojourns were also those who were the
most likely to be satisfied with the academic aspects as well, and
they held more favorable opinions regarding the local people at the
time of this research.

As the last section of this chapter has dealt with generalizations arising from the international intercorrelation of data and some
of the specific implications that may be drawn, any attempt to write
a concluding section to this chapter would be either redundant or
superfluous, or both. Such further comments, where appropriate,
will be placed in the concluding chapter of this book where we have
attempted to summarize, draw conclusions, and point out some of
the policy implications that seem to us to be justified on the basis
of our investigation.

NOTE

1. See W. Frank Hull IV, Foreign Students in the United
States of America: Coping Behavior within the Educational Environment (New York: Praeger, 1978), pp. 96-102, for a further discussion of this in terms of data collected in the United States.

12

SUMMARY AND CONCLUSIONS

It has been the object of this present investigation to gain knowledge that will assist foreign students in making the necessary adjustments to host institutions and cultures. This is important, we feel, in order to increase the chances of positive completion of work for degrees, credentials, or diplomas not only in the countries participating in this investigation but in other countries as well. It is also our feeling that through further understanding, professionals and friends may be better able to assist foreign students during the coping and adaptation process at sojourn institutions and also to help them prepare for their stay even before they leave their homelands. Our goals were ambitious, but our contribution, as represented in this present investigation, must be viewed more modestly. Our investigation was planned and conducted multinationally at all stages, but the best plans are always subject to the realities that exist at the local level at any point along the way.

Working with a team of foreign scholars and researchers in Brazil, Canada, the Federal Republic of Germany, France, Hong Kong, India, Iran, Japan, Kenya, the United Kingdom, and the United States and relying heavily on the local teams' experienced judgments, we have collected data of basically two types with regard to the coping process: (1) statistical data compiled from identical questionnaire instruments completed in the above 11 countries by 2,536 nonimmigrant foreign students, and (2) case study data, more clinical in nature, obtained through a series of longitudinal interviews throughout the first academic year with random samples of foreign students who were arriving at the study institution for their first foreign sojourn in the above 11 countries. We have also included data from the more reflective judgments of those mature scholars who returned from sojourns between 1960 and 1966, 12 or

176

more years earlier (again studied through identical questionnaire instruments and case studies) and were then back in their native countries of Canada, France, Hong Kong, India, Iran, Japan, Kenya, the United Kingdom, and the United States.

For this investigation of the coping process, the statistical data were gathered at the mid-academic year at participating institutions of higher education (during months 5 through 7 of the academic year) between 1976 and 1978. In these countries, the academic calendars varied widely, which accounts in part for the span in calendar years that it took to complete the data collection.

Most of the respondents were males (72.6 percent), on the average 25 years of age (although the average age in the various country samples ranged from 23 years to 27 years), who were seeking first baccalaureate degrees, diplomas, or certificates in a wide variety of disciplinary areas. They came from 139 countries. Most (82.1 percent) had lived mainly in urban areas in the years prior to their sojourn. Furthermore, a large percentage (42.5 percent) had been in the sojourn country for more than two years. Some (26.9 percent) had arrived with no formal education following secondary school, while a group slightly larger (31.0 percent) had completed five or more years of formal study prior to arrival. Most of the respondents (65.8 percent) were living with someone rather than living alone.

Universities often provide special services, materials, and personnel to assist foreign students. For the total population in this investigation, university publications, academic regulations, and so on, were felt to be "satisfactory." On the other hand, the publications had not always been used by most of the respondents. Advisory services specially designed for foreign students had been used by 42 percent of the respondents and were judged to have been "satisfactory" by 70 percent of the users. University counseling services, on the other hand, were used by 25.1 percent and judged "satisfactory" by 64 percent of those users. Those who had not used these services, however, tended to feel that both services would be "satisfactory" (74 percent and 75 percent of the nonusers respectively).

It was found that previous travel on the part of the respondents was associated with better coping skills for the sojourn in question as well as fewer difficulties and problem areas. A relatively small number (20.1 percent) of the respondents had visited the sojourn country for more than one month before their arrival, but almost half (46.4 percent) had visited other foreign countries for continuous periods of more than one month prior to their present sojourn. "Previous travel" in our analysis was defined as a period away from the home country for a continuous stay of at least one month. Those

who had traveled previously (a combined variable from our data
that included 53.9 percent of the total population) had more contact
with local people during their sojourn in a number of ways (see
especially Chapter 11 and throughout). The period of one month
away from the home country, in other words, was an important
factor related to the coping process as our respondents reported on
it. More research could profitably be directed to illuminate further
our understanding of what is actually involved in the variable of
previous travel and whether, in fact, "one month" is the critical
time period to be away from the home country. It is also possible
that those who have traveled already have a friendlier attitude
toward foreign people, and therefore cope more easily with a new
environment.

We found that the expense of housing weighed heavily on the
minds of respondents everywhere. Internationally, 43 percent
found the "excessive expense of housing" to be a problem. "Financial problems" in general were a problem for 41 percent of the respondents. Housing was an area that seemed to contribute to very
serious problems. Housing for foreign students is obviously an
important consideration of which host institutions must be constantly
aware. It must be both available and affordable.

We found a tremendous amount of disappointment and even
discouragement when our respondents were seeking, were open to,
or were expecting more social contact with local students and individuals than they found. We discussed our findings throughout in
terms of a "modified culture contact" hypothesis and are prepared
to argue that: "those foreign students satisfied and comfortable with
their interactions with local people and the local culture during
their sojourn will report broader and more general satisfaction with
their total sojourn experience, both academically and nonacademically." Contact, we are convinced, is a complex variable that in
itself can generate more contact which, in turn, generalizes as a
positive or negative experience throughout the total sojourn. We
are not prepared to argue that contact is the single and most important variable in the transnational coping process, but it is certainly a very important and major variable in that process. The
availability of means and options for social contact, in terms of
what the individual foreign student considers "adequate," is very
important in the coping process in all countries. This is also an
area in which many respondents explicitly indicated that they needed
help both initially and throughout their sojourn.

Respondents in our investigation did show evidences of what
some have called a "foreign student ghetto" pattern. In some
countries the situation was extreme. To illustrate, 63 percent of
the respondents in Iran indicated that their regular contact was with

fellow nationals, as was the case with 60 percent of the respondents
in Japan, 52 percent in France, 50.5 percent in Canada, and so on.
Many respondents indicated clearly that they just did not know how
to go about establishing meaningful relationships with local people
and thus fell back on fellow nationals in order to have someone with
whom to talk and share experiences. A majority of the respondents
(56 percent) indicated that when they were in the company of others,
those others were mainly fellow nationals or other foreign students.
While most respondents said that they had made "good friends"
since arriving in the sojourn country (87.3 percent), many (57 percent) also indicated that their "best friend" in the sojourn country
was either a fellow national or another foreign student. Details
varied by country, as we have indicated throughout our presentation.
For example, in eight of the country samples, the "best friend" was
likely to be a fellow national or another foreign student for at least
half of the respondents. It must, of course, be kept in mind that
this is not to say that the respondents wanted it that way, but this
is a pattern that can be expected to develop (except for those with
"previous travel" experience) without some direct assistance to the
foreign students in helping them establish relations with local individuals and families. Present programming is not adequate in this
respect.

The actual amount of contact shown on behavioral indicators
between our foreign students and local individuals was slight almost
everywhere. To be sure, the respondents were in the sojourn
countries seeking an education and many did indicate that they were
pressed for time (some, one must remember, were experiencing
language difficulties and felt uncomfortable in using the host country's language in social conversation), yet it was clear that more
contact would have been welcomed by most of the students. Positive
contact with their neighbors at their place of residence, the opportunity to discuss significant issues with local individuals, and doing
academic work in cooperation with them were the three most frequent types of social contact reported by the respondents—these
three variables were described as occurring just slightly more than
"sometimes." Other variables categorized as occurring "sometimes" were (a) going for walks, outings, or evenings with local
individuals, (b) opportunities for social contact with local families,
(c) invitations to visit local families, and (d) sharing meals with
local people in their neighborhood. Involvement in community
activities with local individuals and collaborating with them on an
artistic or social activity (for example, theatrical performance,
film club, social action, and so forth) were mentioned as occurring
only "rarely." Our respondents everywhere indicated that they
would like more ways of being involved with local individuals and in

local activities, but they also openly admitted that they required more assistance in these areas.

We considered Robert G. Zajonc's notions of the foreign student as "the stranger" and the "attitudinal aggression" that he feels is likely to be found since the need to conform occurs at the point where difficulties in conforming are great. While Zajonc's conceptualization of the foreign student as "stranger" does introduce a helpful way of understanding some of the coping difficulties facing foreign students, we came to the conclusion that the frustration that is associated with conformity needs seems likely to decrease through positive and satisfying social contact with local individuals and need not necessarily exhibit itself in "attitudinal aggression." Our data did not focus clearly enough on attitudes per se to enable us to make further comment on Zajonc's ideas.

We were unable to locate significant support for the "national status hypothesis" in our data, but we admit that this was not one of the primary foci of our investigation. This hypothesis requires a particularized methodology that we were unable to apply for many reasons.

The "U-curve" hypothesis that has been widely accepted was one object of our investigation. We anticipated obtaining material supporting the hypothesis from the longitudinal case study interviews that were conducted. We also made various detailed analyses of the statistical data to find evidences of the "U-curve" in operation. While the coping process did illustrate initial difficulties related to adaptation to the culture and the milieu of the sojourn institution, these adjustment factors did not follow any "U-curve" pattern. In fact, our analyses found almost no support whatever for the "U-curve" hypothesis within our samples. Support was also noticeably absent in the case studies.

Loneliness and homesickness were found among some of our respondents, but these were not factors that seemed debilitating in themselves. The feeling of having been the object of discrimination was, for our respondents, a more serious matter. Of the total population, 29.3 percent indicated that they felt they had been the object of discrimination, while 39.2 percent indicated that they knew of friends or relatives who had had the experience. The difference in the two items seems to us important: it was easier to locate those who knew of others who had been discriminated against than to find those who felt that they themselves had been the object of discrimination.

We found that personal depression was a problem for a large number of foreign students in all the countries in this investigation. Of the population responding to the item, 25 percent or 639 individual foreign students reported that they had found personal depression to be a source of difficulty for them. Both personal depression and personal discrimination tended to be associated with a host of negative factors and seemed to generalize into an overall negative experience.

The self-reported impact of an educational sojourn experience, if our respondents can be accepted as not unrepresentative of foreign students in general, tends to be in the areas of:

1. intellectual development;
2. personal development;
3. independence;
4. feelings of self-confidence.

Religious attitudes or feelings and political attitudes were the least likely to be reported as having changed as a result of their experience abroad. Certainly our respondents felt that their sojourn was opening up new research interests, ideas, and opportunities (83.7 percent). The long-term impact of the educational sojourn experience was overwhelmingly judged to have been positive by those who had previously participated in such a sojourn 12 or more years earlier.

We were not primarily concerned with the "brain drain," since others were investigating that issue thoroughly. Our data did indicate, however, that relatively few respondents expressed a preference to remain in the sojourn country (14.9 percent) and most wanted to return to their home countries (53.6 percent). Furthermore, in our interviews we were not able to find antecedents of a "brain drain" in the coping process. It was true, however, that the occurrence of certain negative factors in the sojourn experience, such as personal discrimination, was likely to make respondents anxious to leave the sojourn country.

Finally, in terms of the academic and nonacademic aspects of their sojourn, we found the following: with regard to their studies, 27.3 percent of the total population indicated that they were "very satisfied" and 83.1 percent indicated that they were either "satisfied" or "very satisfied." With regard to other aspects of their sojourn, 25.4 percent of the total population indicated that they were "very satisfied" and 77.3 percent indicated that they were either "satisfied" or "very satisfied." Hence our respondents were in general satisfied with both the academic and the nonacademic, including social aspects of their sojourns, but somewhat more frequently with the former.

There were differences in the coping process attributable to the geographic origins of the respondents. After rather detailed and complex analyses in this area, we concluded by pointing out the following: First, students from the Asian countries were more likely to find themselves with non-native students at the sojourn locations. They were also more likely to report personal depression, personal discrimination, and more frequent loneliness. Even though they were more likely to be in frequent contact socially with local individuals, that contact did not seem to make them feel more comfortable with their sojourn or with the difficulties they perceived. In fact, those from the Asian countries together with those from South Asia were the most likely to report considerable dissatisfaction with the nonacademic aspects of their sojourn.

Second, students from the Latin American countries were the most likely to report their experiences and perceptions at one extreme or the other. They seemed to feel that things were either going very well or very poorly for them.

Third, students from the Arabic-speaking countries were likely to report that most of their contact was in the company of other Arabic-speaking students. They were also the most likely to feel that the helpfulness of the teachers was very unsatisfactory; however, those from the United States were even more likely to be dissatisfied with the academic aspects of their sojourns.

Fourth, students from black Africa were likely to be having difficulties and problems during their sojourns. Their concerns, on the other hand, were less widespread or extreme than those presented by students from Asia.

Overall, the factors which were most important with regard to the foreign students' coping process at the foreign university were basically two: social contact with those local to the sojourn culture and area, and prior foreign experience as evidenced by previous travel. Somewhat surprisingly, we did not find that the presence or absence of a local student as a roommate played a very important role in the social contact experiences and feelings of our respondents. The important factor was rather the appropriate access to local individuals. Those who had traveled previously, or those who were fortunate enough to have received assistance in meeting and becoming involved with local people, were also those who presented a generally more positive experience and were more pleased with their experience overall. More research is needed on basic personality factors that may relate to many of these findings.

13

PRACTICAL IMPLICATIONS

At various points throughout this presentation, we have indicated that our analysis of the statistical data and the interviews led to certain conclusions as to what could be done to improve the sojourn of a student or a more senior scholar at a foreign university. In the present chapter we shall attempt a more systematic presentation of the practical implications that emerge from our own research, frequently supported by and rarely in conflict with previous investigations by our colleagues and ourselves; this does not mean, however, that we regard what we have done as merely a replication of previous studies. Not only was our methodology different in many respects but the population we sampled was much more extensive, and was truly international in character. This enables us, we believe, to present the following practical implications with a reasonable degree of assurance, but in certain cases, as indicated below, we regard them as requiring further investigation and experimentation before they can be adequately implemented.

In one sense, it might be said that we ended our investigation where we began, only more so! That is to say, we started out with the conviction that a sojourn at a foreign university should be encouraged, that most participants in such programs were satisfied with them and felt that they had gained a great deal from them, but that there were problems and difficulties which arose in many cases and which might lead to unhappiness and a feeling of failure with regard to the foreign experience in general. We thought that this last outcome would apply to only a minority of cases, but we felt that if possible that minority should be helped to overcome those difficulties. Our conviction along these lines has been strengthened, but we feel that we have learned more about the nature and extent of the problems encountered and more about what can be done about them.

In the presentation that follows we shall make use once again of the chronological or case history approach, starting with the issue of how participants in foreign programs are chosen and ending with what happens when they return home or decide to stay abroad.

The question of selection (or screening) of candidates for a foreign sojourn did not enter specifically into our research design, but we did obtain certain relevant information through our interviews. We were struck in particular by the large variety of motivations expressed by foreign students and the frequency with which "accidental" factors (the availability of a scholarship, the wishes of a parent, the presence in the foreign country of a sibling or other relative, an unhappy personal or political situation at home) played a part in addition to what might be regarded as more reasonable and relevant motives. No screening process can be successfully applied in all cases, since so many foreign students select themselves, but those responsible for the distribution of scholarships would be well advised, in our opinion, to keep the following considerations in mind.

In the first place, those who go abroad should have academic training adequate for entrance into the program at the foreign university in which they plan to enroll. This would seem to be too obvious to require mention, and it is certainly kept in mind by the administrators of many international education programs, but we were struck by the number of foreign students who found their academic background inadequate. The second aspect refers to the personality attributes of the candidates; here the problem is more serious because in the majority of cases it does not enter into the screening process except by chance. It should not be too difficult to identify some of the relevant qualities; openness to new experiences, a positive attitude to cultural differences, ability to make friends without too much difficulty, personal independence and security, flexibility in the solution of new problems—these would probably be included in any list of possible criteria. They almost certainly enter into success abroad at various levels of training. Even in the case of heads of missions in the area of technical assistance (or technical cooperation), failures, when they occur, are occasionally due to professional incompetence, but much more frequently to factors of personality. In the case of married persons, such factors regarding the spouse (so far usually the wife, but in these changing times it may well be the husband) may be equally predictive of success or failure. They deserve much more attention than they have so far received.

There is one aspect of this issue which remains an enigma, and in connection with which our own data throw no light. Apart from motives, good or bad, reasonable or unreasonable, which students consciously identify as responsible for their desire to study abroad, the fact remains that some people like the idea and others do not. What distinguishes those individuals, whether students or faculty, who are eager to go abroad and those who are indifferent or even hostile to the idea? This question, of interest to psychologists and of practical importance to administrators of exchange programs, has not yet been adequately answered.

Once the selection has been made, the problem arises as to how the students or faculty members can best be prepared for their foreign sojourn. The reports by foreign students indicate wide variations among different countries in regard to the information supplied before arrival and what they could expect; in every country there was a substantial minority indicating that such information was inadequate, and in some cases totally lacking. "What to expect" covers a large area, both within and outside the university. It is hardly necessary to list the aspects of university life which can create uncertainty in the mind of the newcomer, and the even larger range of situations in the culture as a whole that may hinder the process of adaptation. In our earlier study, an interesting suggestion was made by our Japanese colleagues, namely that "alumni associations" should be created by those Japanese who had themselves studied abroad in a specific institution, and that the student planning to go to the same university should be directed to one or more of these "alumni" before departure. This would take care, at least to some extent, of the situation that arises when the necessary information is available, but when the student involved is uncertain as to where it might be found.

The information required relates both to the university and to the society as a whole; often it is of such a character that it will not be included in official university publications, and may not be considered important enough to be discussed in the description of the new culture. We mentioned above the difficulty encountered by students, local as well as foreign, to enter into contact with French professors (except at the level of advanced study). This fact would certainly not be found in any French manual of higher education, but it can certainly cause considerable unhappiness. Advance knowledge, as already suggested, will not solve the problem, but it may make adaptation somewhat less traumatic. On the other hand, it has been reported[1] that the informality characteristic of most American universities may be confusing and disturbing to foreign students accustomed to a more "respectful" attitude toward the professor— and no interruptions in class! Surely they would be less confused if they knew about this in advance, and were helped to realize the manner in which an American professor perceived and fulfilled the teaching role in that culture.

As for learning in advance what to expect regarding the culture as a whole, the difficulty of obtaining the necessary information is often greatly magnified. Colleagues in a number of countries are convinced that the trauma of "cultural shock" would certainly be reduced if the foreign student, on arrival, knew more about general norms or standards of behavior. Sometimes the relevant information is gained by the student during his foreign sojourn, but without some preparation, some guidance as to what to look for, that student may remain puzzled and confused. Our interviews with foreign students give ample evidence of this confusion, and of the cultural misinterpretations that may result from lack of knowledge.

A number of books have been written in the attempt to fill this need. At a very popular level, two French writers[2] prepared an entertaining account of what French travelers might encounter abroad, and what would be considered to be good manners in the countries they were likely to visit. Perhaps something similar might be prepared for students. As a matter of fact, several attempts have already been made along these lines, written by Americans for American students who go abroad. Another possibility would be to write a new kind of text based upon interviews with students who have been abroad, and including an account of the difficulties, great and small, which contributed to their "culture shock." This could be useful not only in terms of specific content, but as indicating the kinds of problems that foreign students might be likely to encounter during their stay abroad.

This kind of pre-information, which is of major importance, is often lacking. Attempts have been made to supply it through publications, lectures and discussion groups, contact with "alumni," meetings with foreign student advisors, and so on. In this present investigation, we were not too surprised to find that a number of foreign students (often a substantial proportion) reported inadequate information before arrival. What was more startling was to discover how many indicated difficulty in obtaining the needed information after arrival. This may have been due to their own lack of enterprise, but it is highly probable that in many cases they found it difficult to discover where, and from whom, such information could be obtained. This kind of "information about information" seems to us to be a matter of high priority deserving the attention of administrators of international education programs.

The importance of adequate preparation in the use of the language of the new host country appears to be too obvious to require emphasis, but our own experience during the course of this investigation indicates how important it is to be aware of its implications. Our statistical data and our interviews testify to the frequency with which the lack of proficiency in the host language creates problems. In fact, many of the foreign students themselves spoke of the importance of the language factor, and indicated in the interviews that a single-year sojourn was inadequate in the case of those who had to spend such a large part of it learning to read and write with reasonable proficiency.

As a consequence, we believe it to be desirable to draw the following practical implication. When foreign students plan only a single-year stay in a foreign university, they should be discouraged from coming unless able to demonstrate real competence in speaking and understanding the language of instruction; otherwise, they may have to devote most of the year to the task of acquiring language competence. If on the other hand, the plan is to stay for several years, long enough to obtain a degree or diploma, the loss of time during the first year might be regarded as worth while in view of the long-term goal which is envisaged. An exception should be made for those whose aim is to learn the language and something about the culture. For them, one year might be very valuable.

We have already indicated a number of other problems which foreign students must face upon arrival, and which may cause varying degrees of frustration. The first contacts with the university may be painful if students have difficulty in learning the ropes, the details regarding registering for courses, discovering where to go and when, what library to use, and so on. Similarly, the first contacts with the society may be unhappy if there is trouble finding lodgings which are reasonably satisfactory and not too expensive.

The problem of finding adequate lodging can be one of the most troublesome, as we have indicated in Chapter 6. It is also one of the most difficult to solve. The fact that students vary so much in their tastes and preferences with regard to housing, even apart from differences in financial resources, makes it impossible to set up any housing scheme calculated to satisfy all foreign students. Whatever is done will fail to satisfy some of them. It should be possible, however, to give them more help in finding lodging, in indicating what is available, the feasible alternatives, the costs, the nature of the installations, the people involved, and so forth. Perhaps most important, the foreign students must be protected against having to face discrimination on the part of landlords who dislike the color of their skin. This could be done through the preparation of lists of possible lodgings where students will be spared such an unpleasant experience.

The first contacts at the university appear to be of major importance, and may set the tone for much of what follows. In our discussion of the "U-curve," we had occasion to point out how frequently depression manifested itself in the early stages of the foreign sojourn, in which the manner in which foreign students are received—or neglected—upon arrival may have a significant impact. The role of foreign student advisors is crucial in this connection; unfortunately, they are nonexistent in many countries and at many universities. Sometimes their function is delegated to other members of the administrative or academic staff; in many British universities there are tutors who receive and guide the new arrivals; sometimes—and not rarely—there is no one to take over that responsibility. This is surely an area where something can be done to ensure that the foreign student receives the orientation required. We have also indicated that the more senior scholars assigned to a foreign university may also face serious difficulties on arrival if there is no one to receive them, to help them become integrated, and to indicate to them their duties and responsibilities and what is expected of them during their sojourn. It is difficult to overemphasize the importance of this function, and the serious consequences that may result when no one has been assigned responsibility for it in the new academic environment.

For the student, another hurdle to overcome on arrival refers to the problem of equivalences or "credits" for degrees obtained or courses completed elsewhere. The beginnings that have been made in the direction of establishing such equivalences internationally are promising but require considerable further attention if this, frequently very frustrating, experience is to be replaced by feelings of confidence that the issue will be adequately handled, both at the foreign university and on returning home.

As far as the actual course of the academic sojourn is concerned, it is clear that the issues already raised—selection, preparation, language facility, reception on arrival, feelings of depression, the question of equivalences, and so on—will all continue to exert an important influence. There are, however, other aspects which have been discussed throughout this report and which we believe should be kept in mind in any attempt to improve the conditions of the foreign sojourn.

Some of the difficulties experienced by foreign students, and described in earlier chapters, appear to be inevitable as the result of moving from one academic environment to another. Dislike of the "term" system by students accustomed to a cycle of a full academic year rather than a period lasting only ten weeks; the formality of professors as compared to the informality at home (or vice versa); the difficulty of obtaining information from teachers regarding the students' progress—these and other complaints can hardly be expected to bring about a transformation of the teaching system at a foreign university. What can, however, be done more efficiently is to make clearer to these students what they must expect to find at the new university. In some cases, however, a certain amount of accommodation should be possible. Professors with the reputation of inaccessibility may literally be too busy with large classes, with advanced students, and with their own research to change the pattern of their relations with the newcomers; but it should be possible to arrange for other, possibly junior members of their departments to pay more attention to the needs of the foreign students. It appears highly probable that some proportion of academic failure on the part of foreign students is due to their difficulty in discovering just what was expected of them by their professors.

In earlier chapters (particularly Chapters 4 and 5) we directed considerable attention to the question of contacts with the local population, and the development of friendships with local students. Previous studies have indicated that satisfaction with the foreign experience is closely related to whether the visiting students feel that they have made good friends in the host country, and our own results are in the same direction. We believe that we have gone somewhat further, however, in demonstrating the extent to which the factor of personal contact is intertwined with almost all aspects of the foreign experience. This finding strengthens the widespread conviction that facilitating such contact is crucial to the success of the whole exchange enterprise.

It is not easy to create friendships, but it should be possible to help create an atmosphere in which friendships may more easily develop. A difficulty that often arises is that foreign students may react to programs designed for this purpose as artificial, patronizing, or condescending. Our interviews contain many indications of this attitude, accompanied by the wish to establish contacts on a more natural and informal basis. The patterns of ethnic discrimination still found in many countries toward visitors from certain parts of the world (although probably more rarely at the universities themselves) make the solution of this problem all the more difficult in the case of certain ethnic groups. The issue is complicated by the difficulty of knowing whether to assign responsibility to the hosts, to the visitors, or to both. If to both, it would be useful to know more accurately in what proportions such responsibility is divided, and also how these proportions vary with the characteristics and attitudes of the hosts and visitors respectively.

Most previous research has emphasized mainly the reactions of the visitors, and has tended to neglect those of the host population. Are French students—and others in the local population—more (or less favorable to the presence of foreigners at their universities than are students and others in the United Kingdom or the United States? To what extent do university communities within the same country differ in this respect? What measures are taken (by host families or by the students themselves) to make the foreign students feel a

little more at home, and what indications are there of the success
of such measures? It is difficult to be more specific regarding the
policy implications of this issue, but it is of such capital importance
that at the very least we must urge that more attention be paid to it.
It may be possible, for instance, to make progress in this regard
by enlisting the cooperation of at least a proportion of the local
students, inviting them to play a more direct part in making the
visitors feel at home, and possibly serving as "hosts" or "tutors"
especially in the early stages of the foreign sojourn. We remind
our readers of the point made in the final chapter of the United
States study where it was concluded that "sensitive activists are of
value among foreign student professionals."[3]

Earlier in this report (Chapters 1 and 6) we spoke of the hope
so often expressed by those responsible for exchange programs that
a stay at a foreign university would contribute to better international
understanding, reflected in a more favorable and friendly attitude
toward the host country and its people. The published literature in
this connection is not always in agreement. Morris,[4] for example,
found that most of the foreign students in the United States ended
their sojourn more favorable to that country than when they arrived.
On the other hand, Tajfel and Dawson[5] have made an analysis of
essays written by African, Asian, and West Indian students in the
United Kingdom, and significantly entitled their report Disappointed
Guests. Our own data unfortunately do not give much support to the
view that a sojourn at a foreign university significantly improves
attitudes toward the host country. Attitudes were on the whole
friendly on arrival, but become slightly less so on the average after
a period of residence in nine out of our eleven country samples. In
view of the fact that other investigators have reported more optimistic
results, we shall not insist on the certainty of our own findings, but
at the very least we feel justified in concluding that confidence in a
favorable outcome with regard to international understanding is not
always justified. On the other hand, our demonstration of the manner in which the various factors related to experience at a foreign
university are interrelated allows us to hope that if more attention
is paid to handling the "problems and difficulties" that we have identified, a corresponding improvement in international attitudes may
be expected. It should be added that our retrospective study of
senior scholars indicates a more positive outcome in this respect,
and it is striking to note how frequently the interviews refer to the
importance of a certain "maturity" in candidates for a foreign
sojourn as contributing to the success of the total experience.

With regard to the return home, it is only the retrospective
part of our study which yields pertinent information. As has already
been indicated, a large majority of our respondents felt that the

experience abroad had helped them in their careers, and were in general enthusiastic regarding the positive impact of that experience. The one negative note that was sounded with some frequency related to the difficulty (occasionally the impossibility) of finding a professional opening at home which would permit the further development or application of the new technical skills which had been acquired abroad. This situation raises a number of difficult questions. When governments and foundations grant scholarships, particularly to students from the Third World, how much attention should be paid to whether there are openings at home for the professional competence acquired at a foreign university? Should students be encouraged to develop the technical skills required for their own country's development, and discouraged from becoming specialists in Shakespeare or Descartes? How much should be left to their own free choice? There would probably be no consensus in the answers to these questions, but if the training received abroad is completely irrelevant or inapplicable when the students return, they are faced by a choice between inevitable frustration or remaining abroad.

In our own investigation, a relatively small minority of foreign students expressed the desire to remain permanently in the country in which they were studying, but their sojourn was not yet terminated, and we have no way of knowing what proportion would definitely become part of what is usually called the "brain drain." The decision not to return home is usually considered, and understandably so, as indicating failure in the program, since the foreign students sent abroad fail to bring back the skills which their own country needs, and for the acquisition of which they were given their scholarships in the first place. No one can deny the importance of this argument. On the other hand, a move to another country may mean not only, and not primarily, the chance to increase one's income; it may create the opportunity for gifted individuals to make a significant contribution to the world's knowledge. In addition, the presence of a Chinese physicist in an American laboratory, of an Indian professor at a Canadian university, an African doing research in France, a West Indian physician at a British hospital, may all add to cultural contact and also to international understanding. In our own investigation, those foreign students who expressed a desire to stay rather than to return to their own country always constituted a relatively small minority, and in any case should not necessarily be criticized for their choice. The "brain drain" is not always nor inevitably a sign of failure.

This list of possible practical applications is by no means complete. The material presented in earlier chapters includes mention of a number of other practical issues, sometimes affecting almost all groups of foreign students (for example, finances);

sometimes found in small numbers but in all national samples (for example, serious depression, requiring the intervention of counselors with cross-cultural experience); sometimes restricted to foreign students in certain countries (for example, complaints regarding the inaccessibility of professors). It is important to note that with the variations in the frequency of difficulties encountered in different country samples, the importance of specific practical implications will vary from one country to another. We also remind our readers once again that when our data for a particular country are based on small samples, the results must be considered as hypotheses rather than conclusions. Some of the differences we report between country samples may also in part be due to factors such as the average length of residence in the new country, or the geographical origins of the foreign students rather than the conditions encountered in the country of sojourn. We hope we have made a contribution toward a better understanding of what happens when students attend a foreign university, but a number of significant questions remain unanswered. We shall feel rewarded if what we have done stimulates others to continue and extend the process of discovery.

NOTES

1. Stephen Bochner, "Problems in Culture Learning," in Overseas Students in Australia, ed. S. Bochner and P. Wicks (Sydney: New South Wales University Press, 1972).

2. P. Daninos and E. Ogrizek, eds., Savoir-vivre International (Paris: Odé, 1950).

3. W. Frank Hull IV, Foreign Students in the United States of America (New York: Praeger, 1978), p. 188.

4. R. T. Morris, The Two-Way Mirror: National Status in Foreign Students' Adjustment (Minneapolis: University of Minnesota Press, 1960).

5. H. Tajfel and J. L. Dawson, eds., Disappointed Guests (London: Oxford University Press, 1965).

APPENDIX A
COUNTRY OF CITIZENSHIP:
TOTAL RESPONDENT POPULATION

Countries Represented in the Population	Respondents	Percent
Austria	3	0.1
Belgium-Luxembourg	19	0.8
Denmark	3	0.1
Federal Republic of Germany	44	1.8
Finland	7	0.3
France	66	2.6
Gibraltar	1	0.0
Iceland	7	0.3
Ireland	11	0.4
Italy	19	0.8
Malta	4	0.2
Netherlands	19	0.8
Norway	9	0.4
Portugal-Azores	11	0.4
Spain	8	0.3
Sweden	10	0.4
Switzerland	18	0.7
United Kingdom	94	3.7
Hungary	3	0.1
Poland	15	0.6
Romania	1	0.0
Union of Soviet Socialist Republics	1	0.0
Yugoslavia	10	0.4
Algeria	12	0.5
Botswana	4	0.2
Burundi	1	0.0
Cameroon	4	0.2
Central African Republic	2	0.1
Dahomey	1	0.0
Ethiopia	7	0.3

Countries Represented in the Population	Respondents	Percent
Gabon	2	0.1
Ghana	17	0.7
Guinea	2	0.1
Ivory Coast	9	0.4
Kenya	14	0.6
Lesotho	1	0.0
Liberia	1	0.0
Libya	19	0.8
Malagasy	1	0.0
Malawi	1	0.0
Mali	1	0.0
Mauritius	23	0.9
Morocco	6	0.2
Nigeria	38	1.5
Rhodesia	17	0.7
Rwanda	1	0.0
Senegal	10	0.4
Sierra Leone	4	0.2
South Africa	16	0.6
Sudan	14	0.6
Swaziland	2	0.1
Tanzania	13	0.5
Togo	2	0.1
Tunisia	7	0.3
Uganda	46	1.8
Upper Volta	3	0.1
Zaire	1	0.0
Zambia	2	0.1
Bahrain	7	0.3
Cyprus	8	0.3
Greece	50	2.0
Iran	104	4.1
Iraq	22	0.9
Israel	26	1.0
Jordan	15	0.6
Kuwait	10	0.4
Lebanon	27	1.1
Saudi Arabia	42	1.7
Arabian Peninsula	1	0.0
Syria	3	0.1

Countries Represented in the Population	Respondents	Percent
Turkey	45	1.8
Egypt	38	1.5
Yemen, North and South	7	0.3
Afghanistan	19	0.8
Bangladesh	2	0.1
Sri Lanka	19	0.8
India	99	0.9
Nepal	5	0.2
Pakistan	35	1.4
Australia	27	1.1
Burma	3	0.1
People's Republic of China	3	0.1
Hong Kong-Macao	118	4.7
Indonesia	12	0.5
Japan	62	2.5
Korea	37	1.5
Laos	1	0.0
Malaysia	71	2.8
New Guinea	1	0.0
New Zealand	12	0.5
Philippines	10	0.4
Singapore	13	0.5
Taiwan, Republic of China	102	4.1
Thailand	54	2.1
Vietnam	4	0.2
Argentina	5	0.2
Bahamas	2	0.1
Barbados	**1**	**0.0**
Bolivia	14	0.6
Brazil	39	1.6
Canada	65	2.6
Chile	21	0.8
Colombia	12	0.5
Costa Rica	13	0.5
Cuba	1	0.0
Dominican Republic	1	0.0
Ecuador	7	0.3
El Salvador	10	0.4
Guatemala	3	0.1
Guyana	9	0.4
Haiti	11	0.4

Countries Represented in the Population	Respondents	Percent
Honduras	9	0.4
Jamaica	10	0.4
Mexico	34	1.4
Nicaragua	14	0.6
Panama	35	1.4
Paraguay	20	0.8
Peru	44	1.8
Trinidad	11	0.4
United States	231	9.2
Uruguay	7	0.3
Venezuela	51	2.0
West Indies	21	0.8
Belize	2	0.1
Missing	13	Missing
Total	2,517	100.0

Source: Compiled by the authors.

APPENDIX B
COUNTRY OF CITIZENSHIP:
BY COUNTRY OF SOJOURN

Sojourn Country	Country of Respondents	Respondents	Percent of Country Sample
Brazil	Portugal–Azores	2	1.3
	Spain	1	0.7
	Poland	1	0.7
	Guinea	2	1.3
	Ivory Coast	3	2.0
	Nigeria	5	3.4
	Uganda	1	0.7
	Japan	1	0.7
	Thailand	2	1.3
	Bolivia	12	8.1
	Chile	6	4.0
	Colombia	4	2.7
	Costa Rica	9	6.0
	Ecuador	2	1.3
	El Salvador	5	3.4
	Guatemala	2	1.3
	Honduras	4	2.7
	Mexico	2	1.3
	Nicaragua	8	5.4
	Panama	22	14.8
	Paraguay	19	12.8
	Peru	18	12.1
	Uruguay	5	3.4
	Venezuela	13	8.7
	Total	149	100.0
Canada	Austria	1	0.2
	Belgium–Luxembourg	7	1.1
	Denmark	2	0.3
	Federal Republic of Germany	7	1.1
	France	31	5.0

Sojourn Country	Country of Respondents	Respondents	Percent of Country Sample
	Ireland	4	0.6
	Italy	3	0.5
	Netherlands	6	1.0
	Norway	2	0.3
	Portugal–Azores	2	0.3
	Sweden	1	0.2
	Switzerland	3	0.5
	United Kingdom	40	6.5
	Hungary	1	0.2
	Poland	3	0.5
	Yugoslavia	1	0.2
	Algeria	1	0.2
	Burundi	1	0.2
	Cameroon	3	0.5
	Central African Republic	2	0.3
	Dahomey	1	0.2
	Ethiopia	1	0.2
	Gabon	2	0.3
	Ghana	8	1.3
	Ivory Coast	4	0.6
	Kenya	3	0.5
	Mali	1	0.2
	Mauritius	5	0.8
	Morocco	3	0.5
	Nigeria	12	1.9
	Rhodesia	1	0.2
	Senegal	2	0.3
	Sierra Leone	1	0.2
	South Africa	3	0.5
	Togo	2	0.3
	Upper Volta	2	0.3
	Zaire	1	0.2
	Cyprus	1	0.2
	Greece	18	2.9
	Iran	18	2.9
	Iraq	4	0.6
	Israel	10	1.6
	Jordan	2	0.3
	Lebanon	12	1.9
	Saudi Arabia	2	0.3
	Bahrain	5	0.8
	Turkey	9	1.5

Sojourn Country	Country of Respondents	Respondents	Percent of Country Sample
	Egypt	5	0.8
	Yemen, North and South	1	0.2
	Sri Lanka	1	0.2
	India	17	2.7
	Pakistan	6	1.0
	Australia	6	1.0
	Burma	3	0.5
	People's Republic of China	1	0.2
	Hong Kong–Macao	79	12.7
	Indonesia	7	1.1
	Japan	7	1.1
	Korea	1	0.2
	Laos	1	0.2
	Malaysia	22	3.5
	New Zealand	1	0.2
	Singapore	7	1.1
	Taiwan, Republic of China	4	0.6
	Thailand	3	0.5
	Vietnam	1	0.2
	Argentina	2	0.3
	Bolivia	1	0.2
	Brazil	12	1.9
	Canada	1	0.2
	Chile	2	0.3
	Colombia	1	0.2
	Costa Rica	1	0.2
	Cuba	1	0.2
	Dominican Republic	1	0.2
	Ecuador	1	0.2
	El Salvador	3	0.5
	Guyana	6	1.0
	Haiti	9	1.5
	Jamaica	4	0.6
	Mexico	8	1.3
	Nicaragua	2	0.3
	Panama	2	0.3
	Peru	5	0.8
	Trinidad	2	0.3
	United States	92	14.8
	Venezuela	11	1.8

Sojourn Country	Country of Respondents	Respondents	Percent of Country Sample
	West Indies	21	3.4
	Belize	2	0.3
	Missing	3	Missing
	Total	620	100.0
Federal	Austria	1	2.4
Republic of	Belgium-Luxembourg	1	2.4
Germany	France	8	19.0
	Malta	1	2.4
	Norway	1	2.4
	Switzerland	3	7.1
	United Kingdom	2	4.8
	Greece	2	4.8
	Iraq	1	2.4
	Turkey	2	4.8
	Philippines	1	2.4
	Argentina	1	2.4
	Mexico	1	2.4
	United States	17	40.5
	Total	42	100.0
France	Denmark	1	1.0
	Finland	1	1.0
	Germany	4	4.2
	Italy	1	1.0
	Netherlands	4	4.2
	Spain	1	1.0
	Switzerland	1	1.0
	United Kingdom	2	2.1
	Hungary	1	1.0
	Poland	6	6.3
	Yugoslavia	2	2.1
	Ghana	1	1.0
	Ivory Coast	2	2.1
	Malagasy	1	1.0
	Mauritius	1	1.0
	Morocco	3	3.1
	Senegal	7	7.3
	Tunisia	5	5.2
	Upper Volta	1	1.0
	Greece	3	3.1
	Iran	3	3.1
	Iraq	1	1.0

Sojourn Country	Country of Respondents	Respondents	Percent of Country Sample
	Israel	1	1.0
	Lebanon	4	4.2
	Syria	1	1.0
	Turkey	5	5.2
	Egypt	3	3.1
	Bangladesh	1	1.0
	India	3	3.1
	Australia	1	1.0
	Japan	2	2.1
	New Zealand	1	1.0
	Argentina	1	1.0
	Brazil	6	6.3
	Canada	4	4.2
	Ecuador	1	1.0
	Haiti	1	1.0
	Mexico	1	1.0
	United States	6	6.3
	Missing	2	Missing
	Total	96	100.0
Hong Kong	Belgium–Luxembourg	1	2.4
	Federal Republic of Germany	1	2.4
	Italy	1	2.4
	United Kingdom	2	4.8
	Sri Lanka	1	2.4
	Australia	3	7.1
	Japan	3	7.1
	Korea	1	2.4
	Malaysia	5	11.9
	Canada	4	9.5
	United States	20	47.6
	Total	42	100.0
India	Federal Republic of Germany	1	1.8
	Switzerland	1	1.8
	Kenya	3	5.4
	Mauritius	15	26.8
	Nigeria	2	3.6
	Rhodesia	5	8.9
	South Africa	1	1.8
	Afghanistan	1	1.8

Sojourn Country	Country of Respondents	Respondents	Percent of Country Sample
	Sri Lanka	15	26.8
	Nepal	2	3.6
	Malaysia	7	12.5
	New Zealand	1	1.8
	Singapore	1	1.8
	Missing	1	Missing
	Total	56	100.0
Iran	Federal Republic of Germany	1	1.4
	Italy	1	1.4
	Malta	1	1.4
	United Kingdom	2	2.7
	Ethiopia	1	1.4
	Mauritius	1	1.4
	Sudan	1	1.4
	Tanzania	2	2.7
	Tunisia	1	1.4
	Bahrain	2	2.7
	Iraq	3	4.1
	Jordan	8	11.0
	Lebanon	6	8.2
	Saudi Arabia	1	1.4
	Turkey	4	5.5
	Yemen, North and South	6	8.2
	Afghanistan	16	21.9
	India	1	1.4
	Pakistan	8	11.0
	Indonesia	1	1.4
	Japan	1	1.4
	Malaysia	1	1.4
	United States	4	5.5
		73	100.0
Japan	Hungary	1	3.3
	Sudan	1	3.3
	People's Republic of China	1	3.3
	Hong Kong-Macao	3	10.0
	Indonesia	2	6.7
	Korea	6	20.0
	Malaysia	2	6.7

Sojourn Country	Country of Respondents	Respondents	Percent of Country Sample
	New Zealand	1	3.3
	Singapore	1	3.3
	Taiwan, Republic of China	9	30.0
	United States	2	6.7
	Missing	1	Missing
	Total	30	100.0
Kenya	Ireland	1	1.2
	United Kingdom	1	1.2
	Poland	2	2.4
	Yugoslavia	1	1.2
	Botswana	4	4.8
	Ethiopia	3	3.6
	Lesotho	1	1.2
	Malawi	1	1.2
	Rhodesia	3	3.6
	Rwanda	1	1.2
	Senegal	1	1.2
	South Africa	3	3.6
	Sudan	1	1.2
	Swaziland	2	2.4
	Tanzania	10	11.9
	Uganda	39	46.4
	Zambia	1	1.2
	Japan	2	2.4
	United States	7	8.3
	Total	84	100.0
United Kingdom	Belgium-Luxembourg	5	1.4
	Finland	2	0.5
	France	5	1.4
	Federal Republic of Germany	16	4.4
	Iceland	4	1.1
	Gibraltar	1	0.3
	Ireland	1	0.3
	Italy	6	1.6
	Malta	2	0.5
	Netherlands	7	1.9
	Norway	1	0.3
	Portugal-Azores	4	1.1
	Spain	1	0.3

Sojourn Country	Country of Respondents	Respondents	Percent of Country Sample
	Sweden	6	1.6
	Switzerland	2	0.5
	United Kingdom	2	0.5
	Poland	1	0.3
	Romania	1	0.3
	Yugoslavia	2	0.5
	Algeria	1	0.3
	Ethiopia	1	0.3
	Ghana	2	0.5
	Kenya	7	1.9
	Nigeria	4	1.1
	Rhodesia	5	1.4
	Sierra Leone	2	0.5
	South Africa	6	1.6
	Uganda	2	0.5
	Zambia	1	0.3
	Cyprus	7	1.9
	Greece	19	5.2
	Iran	10	2.7
	Iraq	6	1.6
	Israel	2	0.5
	Jordan	2	0.5
	Lebanon	2	0.5
	Turkey	8	2.2
	Egypt	4	1.1
	Sri Lanka	1	0.3
	India	5	1.4
	Nepal	1	0.3
	Pakistan	5	1.4
	Australia	10	2.7
	Hong Kong–Macao	8	2.2
	Indonesia	1	0.3
	Japan	8	2.2
	Malaysia	19	5.2
	New Zealand	5	1.4
	Philippines	1	0.3
	Singapore	4	1.1
	Thailand	2	0.5
	Brazil	8	2.2
	Canada	14	3.8
	Chile	9	2.5
	Ecuador	1	0.3
	Jamaica	2	0.5

Sojourn Country	Country of Respondents	Respondents	Percent of Country Sample
	Mexico	4	1.1
	Nicaragua	1	0.3
	Panama	1	0.3
	Peru	1	0.3
	Trinidad	3	0.8
	United States	83	22.7
	Uruguay	2	0.5
	Venezuela	6	1.6
	Missing	5	Missing
	Total	370	100.0
United States	Austria	1	0.1
	Belgium-Luxembourg	5	0.5
	Federal Republic of Germany	14	1.5
	Finland	4	0.4
	France	22	2.3
	Iceland	3	0.3
	Ireland	5	0.5
	Italy	7	0.7
	Netherlands	2	0.2
	Norway	5	0.5
	Portugal-Azores	3	0.3
	Spain	5	0.5
	Sweden	3	0.3
	Switzerland	8	0.8
	United Kingdom	43	4.5
	Poland	2	0.2
	Union of Soviet Socialist Republics	1	0.1
	Yugoslavia	4	0.4
	Algeria	10	1.0
	Cameroon	1	0.1
	Ethiopia	1	0.1
	Ghana	6	0.6
	Kenya	1	0.1
	Liberia	1	0.1
	Libya	19	2.0
	Mauritius	1	0.1
	Nigeria	15	1.6
	Rhodesia	3	0.3
	Sierra Leone	1	0.1
	South Africa	3	0.3

Sojourn Country	Country of Respondents	Respondents	Percent of Country Sample
	Sudan	11	1.2
	Tanzania	1	0.1
	Tunisia	1	0.1
	Uganda	4	0.4
	Greece	8	0.8
	Iran	73	7.6
	Iraq	7	0.7
	Israel	13	1.4
	Jordan	3	0.3
	Kuwait	10	1.0
	Lebanon	3	0.3
	Saudi Arabia	39	4.1
	Arabian Peninsula	1	0.1
	Syria	2	0.2
	Turkey	17	1.8
	Egypt	26	2.7
	Afghanistan	2	0.2
	Bangladesh	1	0.1
	Sri Lanka	1	0.1
	India	73	7.6
	Nepal	2	0.2
	Pakistan	16	1.7
	Australia	7	0.7
	People's Republic of China	1	0.1
	Hong Kong-Macao	28	2.9
	Indonesia	1	0.1
	Japan	38	4.0
	Korea	29	3.0
	Malaysia	15	1.6
	New Guinea	1	0.1
	New Zealand	3	0.3
	Philippines	8	0.8
	Taiwan, Republic of China	89	9.3
	Thailand	47	4.9
	Vietnam	3	0.3
	Argentina	1	0.1
	Bahamas	2	0.2
	Barbados	1	0.1
	Bolivia	1	0.1
	Brazil	13	1.4
	Canada	42	4.4

Sojourn Country	Country of Respondents	Respondents	Percent of Country Sample
	Chile	4	0.4
	Colombia	7	0.7
	Costa Rica	3	0.3
	Ecuador	2	0.2
	El Salvador	2	0.2
	Guatemala	1	0.1
	Guyana	3	0.3
	Haiti	1	0.1
	Honduras	5	0.5
	Jamaica	4	0.4
	Mexico	18	1.9
	Nicaragua	3	0.3
	Panama	10	1.0
	Paraguay	1	0.1
	Peru	20	2.1
	Trinidad	6	0.6
	Venezuela	21	2.2
	Missing	1	Missing
	Total	955	100.0

Source: Compiled by the authors.

APPENDIX C
ORIGINS:
GEOGRAPHICAL AREA DIVISIONS

Groupings	Countries Included	Respondents
Western European Countries:	Austria	3
	Belgium–Luxembourg	19
	Denmark	2
	Federal Republic of Germany	41
	Finland	7
	France	47
	Ireland	10
	Italy	16
	Netherlands	15
	Norway	8
	Spain	7
	Sweden	10
	Switzerland	13
	Area totals	198
United Kingdom:	Area totals	63
Eastern European Countries:	Hungary	3
	Poland	15
	Romania	1
	Union of Soviet Socialist Republics	1
	Yugoslavia	10
	Area totals	30

Note: Only respondents listing identical countries of citizenship and birth were utilized in these groupings by origins.

Groupings	Countries Included	Respondents
Black African Countries:	Botswana	2
	Burundi	1
	Cameroon	4
	Central African Republic	2
	Dahomey	1
	Ethiopia	7
	Gabon	2
	Ghana	16
	Guinea	2
	Ivory Coast	8
	Kenya	14
	Liberia	1
	Malagasy	1
	Malawi	1
	Mali	1
	Mauritius	23
	Nigeria	38
	Rwanda	1
	Senegal	9
	Sierra Leone	4
	Sudan	14
	Tanzania	13
	Togo	2
	Uganda	46
	Upper Volta	3
	Zaire	1
	Zambia	2
	Area totals	219
Arabic-speaking Countries:	Algeria	12
	Libya	17
	Morocco	6
	Tunisia	7
	Bahrain	7
	Iraq	22
	Jordan	13
	Kuwait	10
	Lebanon	23
	Saudi Arabia	40
	Arabian Peninsula	1
	Syria	2

Groupings	Countries Included	Respondents
	Egypt	37
	Yemen	7
	Area totals	204
Iran:	Area totals	99
South Asian	India	95
Countries:	Afghanistan	19
	Bangladesh	1
	Sri Lanka	18
	Nepal	5
	Pakistan	29
	Area totals	167
South Pacific	Australia	25
Countries:	New Zealand	9
	Area totals	34
Asian Countries:	People's Republic of China	1
	Hong Kong–Macao	97
	Japan	60
	Korea	37
	Laos	1
	Taiwan, Republic of China	95
	Area totals	291
South East	Burma	3
Asian Countries:	Indonesia	12
	Malaysia	68
	New Guinea	1
	Philippines	10
	Singapore	13
	Thailand	54
	Vietnam	4
	Area totals	165
Latin American	Argentina	5
Countries:	Bolivia	13
	Brazil	35
	Chile	21
	Colombia	12

Groupings	Countries Included	Respondents
	Costa Rica	12
	Dominican Republic	1
	Ecuador	7
	El Salvador	9
	Guatemala	3
	Guyana	9
	Mexico	33
	Nicaragua	14
	Panama	33
	Paraguay	20
	Peru	44
	Uruguay	5
	Venezuela	44
	Area Totals	320
Canada:	Area totals	48
United States:	Area Totals	220

Source: Compiled by the authors.

ABOUT THE AUTHORS

OTTO KLINEBERG, Professor Emeritus of Social Psychology at Columbia University, New York, is presently Visiting Professor, Ecole des Hautes Etudes en Sciences Sociales, Paris, and Director of the International Center for Intergroup Relations. He holds an M.D. degree from McGill University, Montreal, and a Ph.D. degree from Columbia University, New York, plus honorary doctorates from the University of Brazil, Rio de Janeiro; Howard University, Washington; McGill University, Montreal; and Drew University, Madison, New Jersey. Dr. Klineberg has distinguished himself as a world scholar who retains personal concern for students and their development. He has published extensively, including an early text, Introduction to Social Psychology, first published in 1940, that remains in use at colleges and universities throughout the world.

W. FRANK HULL IV is Associate Dean of the Faculty and Director of International Programs at Lewis and Clark College, Portland, Oregon, where he also lectures in psychology. Dr. Hull holds his doctorate from Pennsylvania State University. In addition to working as the Associate Research Educator at the Office of the Chancellor at the University of California at Santa Barbara, he has served as Director of the Center for the Study of Higher Education and Assistant Professor of Higher Education at the Graduate School of the University of Toledo, Toledo, Ohio. His previous publications include numerous works on higher education as well as on international variables in off-campus education. He is the author of Foreign Students in the United States of America: Coping Behavior within the Educational Environment (New York: Praeger, 1978), the U.S. effort that was linked to the present international study.